RESTORING
FISCAL SANITY

D1302572

ALICE M. RIVLIN *and* ISABEL SAWHILL
Editors

RESTORING
FISCAL SANITY
How to Balance the Budget

BROOKINGS INSTITUTION PRESS
Washington, D.C.

JUN 0 6 2006

Copyright © 2004
THE BROOKINGS INSTITUTION
1775 Massachusetts Avenue, N.W., Washington, D.C. 20036
www.brookings.edu

Library of Congress Cataloging-in-Publication data
Restoring fiscal sanity : how to balance the budget / Alice M. Rivlin
and Isabel Sawhill, editors.
   p.   cm.
Includes bibliographical references and index.
ISBN 0-8157-7781-7 (pbk. : alk. paper)
1. Budget—United States. 2. Budget deficits—United States.
3. Government spending policy—United States. 4. Fiscal policy—
United States. I. Rivlin, Alice M. II. Sawhill, Isabel V. III. Title.
HJ2051.B78 2004
352.4'8'0973—dc22   2004004795

9 8 7 6 5 4 3 2
The paper used in this publication meets minimum requirements of the
American National Standard for Information Sciences—Permanence of Paper
for Printed Library Materials: ANSI Z39.48-1992.

Typeset in Sabon

Composition by OSP, Inc.
Arlington, Virginia

Printed by Kirby Lithograph
Arlington, Virginia

Contents

Foreword

Few issues are more crucial to the future of the United States than the fiscal policy of our government, and none is more deeply associated with our core task at Brookings, which is to apply independent analysis to public policy. So this book, edited by Alice Rivlin and Isabel Sawhill, is not only a timely contribution to the public debate—it's also an exemplar of the Institution's mission.

For much of the past hundred years, budget meant deficit. After experiencing a brief period of surpluses at the end of the last century, the federal government is projected to run deficits in the neighborhood of half a trillion dollars a year over much of the next decade. These deficits reflect both rising expenditures, especially for Medicare, Medicaid, and Social Security as the baby boom generation retires, and falling tax revenues related to recently enacted tax cuts. At the same time, the federal government appears to be neglecting key areas, including health care for the nonelderly, education, the environment, and the plight of low-wage workers and their children. The nation thus faces a crucial choice: continue down the path of future fiscal irresponsibility while underinvesting in critical areas or increase resources in high-priority areas while also reducing the overall budget deficit. This choice will materially affect Americans' economic well-being and security in the immediate future as well as over longer horizons.

Concerned about this prospect, Brookings last year launched a project we call "Budgeting for National Priorities." This volume is the first product of that effort. Alice and Belle have assembled a book that presents three plans for reducing the deficit over the next ten years: one that emphasizes spending cuts, one that emphasizes tax increases, and one that includes a mixture of both. For the longer term, the project will address the nation's fiscal future in new and more creative ways. Although the currently projected fiscal gap is clearly a problem, it also creates an opportunity to rethink what government does and how we pay for it. Old programs rarely die, some are growing at unsustainable rates, and many serve very narrow if powerful interests or involve the federal government in activities better performed by states or the private sector. The long-term fiscal gap will almost surely put downward pressure on spending. It is important that those pressures be directed toward eliminating ineffective or unnecessary programs and not just those with little political clout—what David Stockman once called "weak claims rather than weak claimants." Similarly, the fiscal gap will generate a new debate about revenues. Quite apart from the revenues it produces, the existing tax system imposes enormous administrative burdens on businesses and households, is badly in need of simplification, and is not well designed to encourage growth and efficiency. Moreover, questions about who is paying what share of the tax burden continue with little agreement about either the facts of the matter or the criteria by which disputes should be resolved.

In the meantime, these issues are getting plenty of short-term attention as well. As the presidential election campaign moves into high gear, this book offers some benchmarks for citizens, commentators, and members of the policy community as they make up their own minds; it will, we hope, help reframe the debate, focusing all participants on the need for painful and politically difficult choices about what government does and how we pay for it. The concrete deficit reduction plans put forth here provide a number of ideas that policymakers may want to adopt while also underscoring the political difficulties involved.

Above all, what's needed if the United States is going to manage its fiscal affairs wisely, with a view to the responsibility of today's leaders for tomorrow's citizens, is a combination of focus and honesty. Both are to be found in abundance in the pages that follow.

STROBE TALBOTT
President

January 2004
Washington, D.C

Acknowledgments

B rookings is grateful to the Annie E. Casey Foundation for its early support of this project but acknowledges that the findings and conclusions presented here are those of the authors alone and do not necessarily reflect the opinions of the foundation.

The editors wish to thank Robert Litan for encouraging them to undertake this effort. They are particularly grateful to the authors for their willingness to produce these chapters on short notice and in the midst of the many other demands on their time. These authors include Henry Aaron, Lael Brainard, William Gale, Ron Haskins, Michael O'Hanlon, Peter Orszag, and Charles Schultze. Not all authors of this project agree with every idea presented here. Some would favor a tougher fiscal policy, others less constrained deficit targets. In addition, not all agree with the specific proposals in the individual chapters, even in cases where they are the principal authors of the chapters in question. (For example, O'Hanlon believes the central defense budget projection in his chapter with Brainard, while plausible, is optimistic in light of likely security requirements in the next decade.) Thus the three options presented here are designed both to give readers several choices and to reflect the sometimes divergent views of the various authors.

The editors also appreciate the advice and guidance of the advisory committee whose members are listed separately at the end of the volume. Helpful advice was also received from Gordon Adams, William Hoagland, Tom Loveless, Paul Portney, Robert Reischauer, Susan Rice, Allen Schick, Gene Steuerle, James Steinberg, and Van Ooms. Finally, special thanks are due to Simone Berkowitz, Melissa Cox, and Una Lee for their research assistance; Brenda Szittya for editing; Andrea Kane, Margy Waller, and Julie Clover for outreach; Nicholas Warren for research verification; Larry Converse, Mary Techau, and Janet Walker for production of the volume; and Jennifer Ambrosino and Evelyn Taylor for administrative assistance.

Executive Summary

Federal spending and taxation have a large impact on the economy and on the lives of individuals and families. Good budget choices can strengthen the economy; bad choices can weaken it. Decisions about the federal budget are always difficult. People differ on what government should do and how to pay for it. Some people believe that the federal government should do more, others less. Many believe that government spending priorities are wrong or that taxes are burdensome or unfair. People also differ on how much deficits matter and on how quickly they need to be addressed.

One fact is indisputable: the federal government is spending about $500 billion a year more than it is raising in taxes. On reasonable assumptions, the gap will widen to nearly $700 billion a year by 2014 and accelerate rapidly thereafter, as the baby boom generation begins to retire.

This book argues that deficits matter a lot and that better policies are possible and urgently needed. Not all budget deficits are harmful—indeed, recent deficits have ameliorated the recession that began in 2001.

However, large persistent deficits weaken the economy and lower family incomes. The authors also believe that passing on large and unnecessary fiscal burdens to future generations is unfair and irresponsible. More specifically, deficits are harmful for five reasons:

—*They slow economic growth.* By 2014, the average family's income will be an estimated $1,800 lower because of the slower income growth that results when government competes with the private sector for a limited pool of savings or borrows more from abroad.

—*They increase household borrowing costs.* A family with a $250,000 thirty-year mortgage, for example, will pay an additional $2,000 a year in interest.

—*They increase indebtedness to foreigners,* which is both expensive and risky. The United States is the largest net debtor in the world. The income of Americans will ultimately be reduced by the interest, dividends, and profits paid to foreigners who have invested in the United States. Moreover, if foreigners lose confidence in the American economy—or begin to worry that we are not managing our fiscal affairs responsibly— they may reduce their investment here. This can reduce the value of the dollar and raise the prices we have to pay for imported goods. If the fall in the dollar were precipitous, it could cause rapid increases in interest rates, possibly recession, or even a serious financial crisis.

—*They require that a growing proportion of revenues be devoted to paying interest on the national debt,* estimated to increase by $5.3 trillion over the next decade. By 2014 this increase in government borrowing will cost the average household $3,000 in added interest on the debt alone.

—*They impose enormous burdens on future generations.* Today's children and young adults and their descendants will have to pay more because this generation has chosen to be irresponsible. Meanwhile, deficits and rising interest costs are likely to put downward pressure on spending for education, nutrition, and health care that could make today's children more productive and thus better able to pay these future obligations.

The budget challenge is daunting, but not impossible to address. The United States is a wealthy, resourceful country that has solved plenty of tough problems before. In a democracy, it is important to identify alternative courses of action that might appeal to different groups and try to find a compromise that all can agree on. In an effort to stimulate that debate, this book presents three alternative ways of balancing the federal budget over the next ten years. We offer one set of choices that might appeal to those who believe that the federal government should be smaller and another to those who believe it should do more. We also present, in more detail, a budget that keeps government the same size but makes it more effective. This plan contains enough spending reduction to achieve balance in ten years, while preserving room for some high-priority new initiatives.

In presenting these alternative budgets, our goals are threefold. First, we show that balancing the budget is feasible (although politically difficult). Second, we show the implications of different strategies that are normally discussed only in general terms. Third, we aim to stimulate a more honest and informed debate about the pros and cons of various fiscally responsible choices in the hopes that others will offer their own detailed proposals for achieving fiscal balance.

The Budget Outlook

Less than three years ago, in fiscal year 2001, the federal budget was running a surplus of $127 billion. But a weak economy, tax cuts, spending increases, and lack of concern for fiscal discipline turned the surplus into a deficit of almost $400 billion in 2003, and the deficit is expected to be even larger in 2004. This shift in federal finances from deficit to surplus would not be a serious concern if it were temporary. Unfortunately, however, the current deficits are projected to continue for the next decade, rising to an estimated $687 billion in 2014. Indeed, if the temporary surpluses in Social Security, Medicare, and federal retirement programs were not masking the size of the deficits in the rest of the budget, the deficit estimate for 2014 would exceed $1 trillion.

Budget Assumptions

The adjusted baseline projections in table 1 show larger deficits than the most recent official projections of the Congressional Budget Office, but that is because the CBO is required by Congress to assume that current law remains unchanged. The tax reduction legislation enacted in 2001, 2002, and 2003 was designed to minimize the appearance of revenue loss associated with the tax cuts by phasing the cuts in slowly and making them expire within ten years. Congress also chose to ignore the fact that the tax changes would subject millions of additional taxpayers to the alternative minimum tax (AMT). In making our adjusted baseline projections, we assumed that Congress will extend temporary tax provisions now on the books and make the 2001, 2002, and 2003 tax changes permanent, and that Congress will amend the alternative minimum tax to prevent an increase in the number of taxpayers subject to the AMT. We also assumed discretionary spending increases in line with population growth as well as with inflation—that is, real discretionary spending per person is held constant—and added the cost of the prescription drug benefit and other changes in Medicare enacted at the end of the first session of the 108th Congress. To be clear, we are not advocating any of these proposals; we are simply assuming that they will be enacted. These assumptions could turn out to be wrong, but they seem more probable than the assumptions underlying the CBO projections.

Deficits beyond 2014

A major additional reason for concern about continuous large deficits is that pressures on the budget are certain to escalate rapidly in subsequent decades, as the baby boom generation retires and longevity continues to increase. The CBO projects that even if medical care costs rise only 1 percent faster than per capita GDP—an optimistic assumption in view of recent increases—expenditures for providing existing benefits under Social Security, Medicare, and Medicaid would rise from 9.0 percent of GDP in 2010 to 14.3 percent in 2030 and to 17.7 percent in 2050. These exploding future costs highlight the need to address the challenge of reforming these entitlement programs as soon as possible. They also make clear the importance of fiscal policy that contributes to future economic growth by enhancing national saving—not reducing both growth and saving by running continuous deficits over the coming decade.

Table 1. Adjusted Baseline Budget, Fiscal Years 2003–14
Billions of dollars

Item	2003	2004	2005	2006
Adjusted spending	2,171	2,312	2,423	2,559
Adjusted revenue	1,770	1,821	1,988	2,129
Adjusted deficit	–374[a]	–491	–435	–430
Excluding Social Security, Medicare, and federal retirement	–590	–711	–669	–665

Item	2007	2008	2009	2010
Adjusted spending	2,709	2,872	3,034	3,199
Adjusted revenue	2,260	2,393	2,535	2,678
Adjusted deficit	–449	–479	–499	–521
Excluding Social Security, Medicare, and federal retirement	–695	–739	–773	–806

Item	2011	2012	2013	2014
Adjusted spending	3,386	3,530	3,745	3,954
Adjusted revenue	2,810	2,949	3,119	3,267
Adjusted deficit	–576	–581	–626	–687
Excluding Social Security, Medicare, and federal Retirement	–872	–888	–930	–1,003

a. See note 3 at the end of chapter 1.

Can Growth Solve the Problem?

Deficits are very sensitive to the rate of economic growth. Should the economy grow faster than the 3 percent rate, in real terms, assumed by the CBO and most private forecasters, deficits will be smaller. If the economy grows more slowly than this, they will be still larger. Some believe that recent changes in tax law will lead to a higher rate of economic growth. But, as detailed in chapter 1 of this book, as long as these tax cuts are deficit financed, the weight of professional opinion suggests that they will not lead to higher growth.

Table 2. *Illustrative Changes in 2014, by Plan Type*
Billions of dollars

Item	Smaller government plan	Larger government plan	Better government plan
Total deficit reduction	687	687	687
Interest payment reduction	−153	−153	−153
Tax increase	134	629	401
Programmatic spending net change	−400	95	−134
Defense net change	0	−60	−60
Increase	0	0	0
Decrease	0	−60	−60
Non-defense net change	−400	155	−74
Increase	0	185	41
Decrease	−400	−30	−115

Source: See table 2-1 in chapter 2.

Three Different Ways of Getting to Balance

In the hope of stimulating serious debate about how to balance the budget, we constructed three alternative plans that differ in the mix of spending cuts and revenue increases used to achieve balance in ten years (table 2). We call them the smaller government plan, the larger government plan, and the better government plan. All three start from our adjusted baseline projections, which indicate that in the absence of policy change, the deficit in 2014 will be about $687 billion (this estimate and others in the tables are based on the CBO's August 2003 report, adjusted as described above. The CBO revised its forecast in December 2003, but the revisions do not materially affect our analysis).

Balancing the unified budget by 2014 will produce interest savings of around $153 billion, leaving a deficit of $534 billion to be eliminated by spending reductions or revenue increases in that year. If we chose the more stringent criterion of balancing the budget excluding the federal retirement programs, additional deficit reduction of $316 billion would be necessary. Although achieving the larger goal would be desirable, as the plans amply illustrate even meeting the less ambitious target requires tough choices that are sure to be unpopular.

Table 3. *Smaller Government Plan*

Item	Billions of dollars
Total deficit reduction	687
Minus debt service savings	−153
Subtotal	534
Plus funding for new initiatives	0
Total: tax increases and spending cuts to eliminate deficit	534
Changes in the budget	
Revenue change	134
Spending cuts	−400
Commercial subsidies	−138
Devolution	−123
Wasteful spending	−7
Non-defense discretionary	−58
Entitlement	−74

Source: See table 2-2 in chapter 2.

The Smaller Government Plan

The smaller government plan would reduce total spending as a share of GDP from 20.2 percent in 2003 to 18.3 percent in 2014. It balances the budget primarily by cutting $400 billion from projected domestic spending in 2014 (table 3). These cuts are achieved by reducing government subsidies to commercial activities ($138 billion); by returning responsibility for education, housing, training, environmental, and law enforcement programs to the states ($123 billion); by slowing the growth of other non-defense discretionary spending ($58 billion); by cutting entitlements such as Medicaid, Social Security, and Medicare ($74 billion); and by eliminating some wasteful spending in these entitlement programs ($7 billion). Revenue increases of $134 billion are added to the package, primarily by raising the gas tax, by lowering but not repealing the estate tax, and by better enforcement of existing tax laws. Although tax increases are unpopular with those who favor smaller government, no one has suggested how to achieve balance without them. Moreover, the revenue measures included in this plan are relatively modest, they are focused on compliance with existing laws, and they avoid changes in the tax rates or brackets enacted in 2001 and 2003.

Table 4. *Larger Government Plan*

Item	Billions of dollars
Total deficit reduction	687
Minus debt service savings	−153
Subtotal	534
Plus funding for new initiatives	95
Total: tax increases and spending cuts to eliminate deficit	629
Changes in the budget	
Revenue change	629
Spending cuts	−90
Defense	−60
Non-defense	−30
New spending	185
Health	100
Education	60
Other	25
Net increase in spending	95

Source: See table 2-9 in chapter 2.

The Larger Government Plan

The larger government plan would increase total spending as a share of GDP from 20.2 percent in 2003 to 20.9 percent in 2014. This increase occurs partly because some existing programs are slated to grow rapidly over the coming decade, as the population ages and the costs of health care rise, and partly because the plan includes additional spending for health care, education, and some other priorities that are only partially offset by savings in existing programs (table 4). To both pay for this new spending and balance the budget requires that taxes be raised substantially. A package of revenue measures that would accomplish this objective is described in chapter 6 of this book. It includes scaling back the 2001 tax cuts that benefited the affluent, eliminating the Social Security earnings ceiling so that all earnings would be taxable, and creating a new value-added tax that would affect almost everyone.

The Better Government Plan

The better government plan is based on the assumption that government has a positive role to play in improving people's lives but could perform this function far more effectively than it does at present. What distinguishes the better government plan from the other two is that instead of changing the size of government, it reallocates spending in ways designed to improve government performance. In addition, this third plan is likely to be more politically feasible than the other two over the next few years, no matter what the outcome of the 2004 election. Whoever is elected president in that year will face a huge fiscal hole that cannot realistically be filled by spending cuts or revenue increases alone. A very substantial amount of both will be needed.

Chapters 3 through 5 of this book discuss the specific restructuring called for by the better government plan to meet international responsibilities (chapter 3), to meet domestic responsibilities (chapter 4), and to honor essential commitments to the elderly or those who are about to retire (chapter 5).

While the authors generally prefer the better government plan, it should be emphasized that not every author agrees with every aspect of the plan. Some authors prefer aspects of the smaller or larger government plans to aspects of the better government plan. Indeed, our disagreements on such matters reflect, in microcosm, the disagreements in the country at large. Nonetheless, we have all taken seriously the desirability of balancing the budget while simultaneously trying to make government more effective. The overall plan is summarized in table 5.

In the national security area, the authors of chapter 3 argue, the United States can use the tools of hard power (military force), soft power (diplomacy and foreign assistance), and domestic counterterrorism (homeland security). These tools are complementary and the budget for national security is best viewed as a unified whole. The better government plan calls for cuts in defense spending. But these are only possible because it is assumed that the reconstruction of Iraq will have been completed by 2014. However, the world is likely still to be a dangerous place in 2014, defense costs per uniformed member of the armed forces have generally

Table 5. *Better Government Plan*

Item	Billions of dollars
Total deficit reduction	687
Minus debt service savings	−153
Subtotal: tax increases and spending cuts to eliminate deficit	534
Plus funding for new initiatives	41
Total: tax increases and spending cuts to eliminate deficit	575
Changes in the budget	
Revenue change	401
Spending cuts	−175
Defense	−60
Social Security, Medicare, and Medicaid	−47
Other domestic	−68
New spending	41
Foreign affairs	11
Homeland security	9
Other domestic	21
Net decrease in spending	−134

Source: See table 2-10 in chapter 2.

risen by 2 to 3 percent a year in real terms, major weapons systems are aging and need to be modernized, and health care costs for military personnel are rising rapidly. Thus containment of defense spending to the levels assumed in this plan will only be possible if weapons modernization is very selective, if privatization of military support operations is more cost effective than it has been in the past, and if it proves feasible to share more of the defense burden with our allies.

While some cuts in defense spending are possible under this scenario, more spending on homeland security and foreign assistance is called for. In the wake of 9/11, air travel is safer, more intelligence is being shared, and ports and public infrastructure are better protected, but additional steps are needed in these areas as well as in some others, such as protecting private infrastructure (chemical plants and trucking, for example). Finally, U.S. foreign assistance is arguably as important as military power in making the world a safer place. This assistance should be increased, but it could be allocated and organized far more effectively than at present. Chapter 3 calls for more to be spent on stimulating economic development and reducing world poverty.

In the domestic arena, the authors of chapter 4 suggest, it is possible to trim spending on existing domestic programs sufficiently to both fund some new initiatives and contribute savings toward the goal of balancing the budget. They call for modest additional outlays in a number of areas, such as restructuring the safety net to encourage and reward work, improving preschool opportunities for disadvantaged children, extending health care coverage to lower-income families, and helping states fund the costs of the extensive testing and teacher training required by the No Child Left Behind Act of 2001. These kinds of public investments, if appropriately structured, can increase productivity and growth as much as or more than private investments in new technologies, facilities, and equipment, while simultaneously opening up opportunities for everyone to participate more fully in a stronger economy. The authors also call for more attention to energy efficiency and a clean environment, but note that this need not increase budgetary costs. The best way to achieve these goals is to use taxes or a system of auctioned and tradable emissions permits to align the price of energy use with its social costs. The added revenue can then be used to help close the fiscal gap.

To fund the new initiatives and contribute savings toward balancing the budget, chapter 4 offers a menu of spending cuts that are far more selective than those discussed in the smaller government plan. But like the smaller government plan, it attempts to identify programs that provide unwarranted assistance to commercial activities (for example, farm subsidies) or state and local governments (for example, construction grants for wastewater and drinking water). It also includes cuts in programs that have not produced benefits commensurate with their costs (for example, manned space flight) and in programs that could be more efficiently administered (for example, student loans).

Chapter 5 addresses three large and rapidly growing programs: Social Security, Medicare, and Medicaid. The authors show that these programs are badly in need of long-term reforms, which will be less disruptive if made quickly. However, since significant cuts in benefits for those already retired or approaching retirement age are not desirable, such reforms will produce few budgetary savings over the next decade. Nonetheless, some savings are identified, primarily from accelerating (to 2012) implementation of the already enacted increase in the retirement age under Social

Security, from more accurate inflation adjustments to Social Security benefits, and from increased premiums for Medicare.

Despite its reliance on a number of very controversial spending cuts, the better government plan necessarily depends heavily on revenue increases to achieve balance in 2014. As noted in chapter 6 of this book, revenues as a share of GDP fell from 20.8 to 16.5 percent between 2000 and 2003. For this reason, all three plans—including the smaller government plan—must use revenue increases to fill at least some of the fiscal gap. The better government plan relies on revenue increases to fill 75 percent of this gap. The biggest increases in revenue come from returning the top four income tax rates to 2000 levels, raising the Social Security earnings ceiling so that 90 percent of earnings are taxable, repealing the 2003 capital gains and dividend tax reductions, and retaining the estate tax with a higher exemption. Throughout this book we refer to these changes as tax *increases*, but many are only increases relative to the adjusted baseline presented in chapter 1. Compared with the official tax code, which assumes that the tax cuts enacted in 2001, 2002, and 2003 will expire in 2010 or before, for most people the changes will still result in a tax *reduction*.

Improving the Budget Process

As chapter 2 of this book argues, reform of the budget process is essential to restoring fiscal discipline. Budget process reform should involve at least three elements: first, caps on discretionary spending that extend for ten years; second, PAYGO rules requiring that any tax cut or increase in mandatory spending be fully "paid for" by offsetting spending or tax changes over a ten-year period, and that these changes normally not be assumed to sunset; and third, a stricter definition of "emergency spending." While process reform alone will not restore fiscal responsibility, it can stiffen the resolve of politicians to do the right thing and provide political cover for resisting deficit-increasing actions.

Conclusion

The authors of this book believe that the nation's fiscal situation is out of control and could do serious damage to the economy in coming decades, sapping our national strength, making it much more difficult to respond to unforeseen contingencies, and passing on an unfair burden to future generations. Yet no one in a political position to do something about this situation has so far come up with an adequate solution. The purpose of this volume is to document the enormity of the problem, to inform citizens about why deficits matter, to suggest the kinds of specific steps that need to be taken, and to challenge others to do the same.

1

Growing Deficits and
Why They Matter

ALICE M. RIVLIN AND
ISABEL SAWHILL

This book is about the difficult choices that citizens and policymakers must make about the priorities in the federal budget. Its basic theme is: we can't have everything; we have to choose what we want most and how we want to pay for it. Right now, we are trying to have it all: lower taxes *and* increased spending—for Social Security, Medicare, defense, homeland security, and many other programs. The result is a government budget that is out of control and that poses substantial risks to the future. Our government is now borrowing about half a trillion dollars a year. But the important point is that there is no end in sight to this tide of red ink. In fact, matters will get far worse once the baby boom generation begins to retire. If nothing is done, the national debt is projected to increase by $5.3 trillion in the next decade alone. The interest on this extra borrowing will cost the average household $3,000 a year, and the economic effects of the deficits will also lower its income by an estimated $1,800.

The authors are indebted to William Gale and Peter Orszag for much of the analysis in the chapter and for their comments on an earlier version.

To be sure, budget projections are very uncertain. They depend on what happens to the economy, on future spending and taxing actions of Congress, and on unpredictable events at home and abroad. No one can claim to know exactly what the future will bring. But intelligent decisions must be based on the most realistic projections that can be made—otherwise they are just blind guesses.

In this chapter we lay the groundwork for the alternatives presented in the rest of the book. We show that on reasonable assumptions about the economy the federal budget is likely to run persistent deficits that reach about $700 billion a year by the end of the decade and remain at 3 percent or more of GDP. These deficits would be much larger—about 5 percent of GDP—if not offset by short-term surpluses in the major federal retirement programs, Social Security and Medicare. But we know that the short-term surpluses in these retirement accounts will soon turn into deficits as the baby boom retires, creating an unprecedented and unsustainable fiscal gap that grows larger and larger over the next few decades. The right time to address this problem is now. The longer we wait to get our fiscal house in order, the greater the risks to the economy and the more painful the solutions will be.

An Overview of the Federal Budget

In 2003, the federal government spent $2.2 trillion. Over two-fifths of this spending was for just three large programs: Social Security, Medicare, and Medicaid (figure 1-1).[1] About a third of current spending is for other (primarily) domestic programs—everything from unemployment insurance and farm subsidies to national parks, education, and programs for the poor. Many of these programs are funded through the annual appropriations process and as a result are referred to as "discretionary," since the funding for them is less automatic than spending on "mandatory" programs, such as Social Security or unemployment insurance. Finally, a significant chunk of the budget goes for defense (19 percent) and for interest on the debt (7 percent).

Total revenues to support these activities fell short of total spending by $374 billion in 2003.[2] These revenues come from personal and corporate

Figure 1-1. *Federal Spending, 2003 Projection*

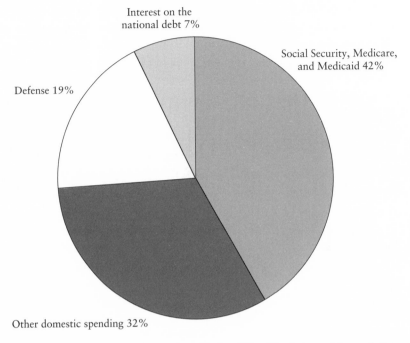

Interest on the
national debt 7%

Social Security, Medicare,
and Medicaid 42%

Defense 19%

Other domestic spending 32%

Source: Author's calculations and Congressional Budget Office, "The Budget and Economic Outlook: An Update," August 2003.

income taxes, from payroll taxes, and from other smaller sources, such as excise and estate taxes (figure 1-2). Over the past few decades the share of expenditures being financed by payroll taxes on workers and employers has grown, while the share being financed by taxes on income has shrunk.[3]

After declining for many years as a share of all outlays, the defense budget is slated to grow along with spending for homeland security, both of which are of greatly increased importance in the wake of 9/11 and the war in Iraq. Domestic discretionary programs have been shrinking as a share of total spending and will probably continue to shrink for the foreseeable future.[4] The three big entitlement programs (Social Security, Medicare, and Medicaid), however, are growing rapidly. Indeed, expected growth in these programs, along with projected increases in interest on

Figure 1-2. *Federal Revenue Sources, 2003 Estimate*

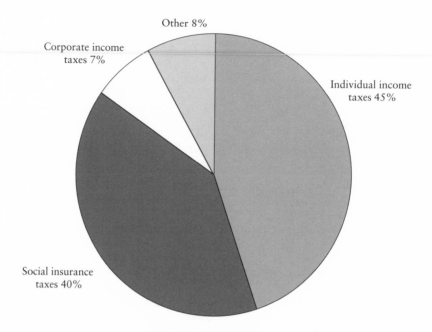

Source: Congressional Budget Office, "The Budget and Economic Outlook: An Update," August 2003.

the debt and defense, will absorb all of the government's currently projected revenue within eight years, leaving nothing for any other program (figure 1-3).

Although the composition of federal spending has shifted over time, with more money being devoted to paying benefits to the elderly and less to other purposes, the overall size of government relative to the economy has changed little and remains at roughly 20.8 percent of GDP.

Where the Deficits Came From

In the 1980s federal deficits grew to worrisome proportions and appeared to be damaging the performance of the economy and confidence in the government's ability to manage its fiscal affairs. Public concern over

Figure 1-3. *The Big Squeeze*

Percent of GDP

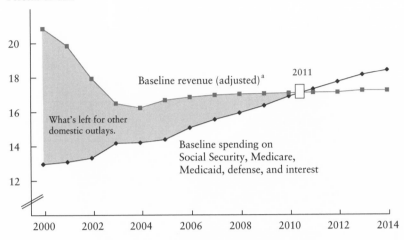

Source: Eugene C. Steuerle, 2003. "The Incredible Shrinking Budget for Working Families and Children," National Budget Issues Policy Brief 1 (Washington: Urban Institute, 2003).

a. Baseline revenue is adjusted to extend expiring tax provisions and to reform the alternative minimum tax.

mounting deficits led politicians of both parties to support aggressive measures to bring them down. President George H. W. Bush worked with a Democratic Congress to pass a budget reduction agreement in 1990. President Bill Clinton dealt with a Democratic Congress in 1993 and a Republican one in 1997 to pass major deficit-cutting packages. These measures, which required many painful compromises, restrained spending and increased revenues. With the assistance of a rapidly growing economy in the 1990s, deficits fell and turned into substantial surpluses by the end of the decade.

But now the surpluses are gone. A weaker economy, tax cuts, and spending increases (especially for defense and homeland security) combined to turn surpluses into deficits again. Revenues fell to 16.5 percent of GDP in 2003, well below the average of recent decades, while spending grew to 20.2 percent of GDP, opening up a deficit gap of 3.7 percent of GDP in 2003.

At the same time, projections of the federal budget outlook have gone through enormous swings from surplus to deficit in the past few years. As recently as early 2001, the Congressional Budget Office was projecting large surpluses in the federal budget, aggregating $5.6 trillion over ten years. Now our adjusted projections (explained below) show that these aggregate surpluses have disappeared and been replaced by aggregate deficits over the next ten years of $5.3 trillion. To the average person these wild swings seem incomprehensible and suggest that no projections should be taken seriously.

There is, however, no mystery about how projected surpluses turned into projected deficits so quickly. The reasons are (1) the recession of 2001 and the slow recovery, (2) tax cuts, (3) increased spending, and (4) more realistic assumptions about future budget policy. Although the recession was the primary culprit in 2002, most of the deterioration in the budget projections between 2002 and 2010 is caused by the recent tax cuts and associated increases in interest on the debt.

The Budget Course for the Next Ten Years

At least twice a year, the Congressional Budget Office publishes baseline projections of the federal budget for Congress to use in making budget decisions. These projections are designed to provide a neutral answer to the question: what will happen to federal spending and revenues if current laws and policies remain unchanged? Congress prescribes certain rules that the CBO must follow in making baseline projections—for example, the CBO is not allowed to assume that most expiring tax provisions will be extended, even if they deem the extensions highly probable. These rules must be kept in mind in interpreting the projections.

The CBO's August 3, 2003, projections show the budget deficit increasing in fiscal years 2003 and 2004 but declining thereafter and reaching a surplus of more than $200 billion by the end of ten years (table 1-1). (The CBO revised its forecast in December 2003, but the revisions do not materially affect our analysis.) The CBO projections assume that the current economic recovery continues and that real GDP grows by an average of 3 percent a year. This is a reasonable economic forecast, roughly in line with the average views of private forecasters. We will explore below the effects of faster growth on future deficits.

Table 1-1. CBO Baseline and Adjusted Baseline, 2003–14

Billions of dollars

	2003	2004	2005	2006	2007	2008	2009	2010	2011	2012	2013	2014
CBO baseline												
Defense	407	452	472	481	489	506	519	533	552	558	578	599
Appropriated spending	419	448	460	467	479	491	502	515	528	542	556	570
Mandatory spending	1,188	1,250	1,289	1,333	1,401	1,482	1,570	1,665	1,776	1,854	1,984	2,104
Subtotal: spending excluding interest	2,014	2,150	2,221	2,281	2,369	2,479	2,591	2,713	2,856	2,954	3,118	3,273
Net interest	157	155	184	220	255	282	301	312	318	316	305	291
Total spending	2,171	2,305	2,405	2,501	2,624	2,761	2,892	3,025	3,174	3,270	3,423	3,564
Revenue	1,770	1,825	2,064	2,276	2,421	2,564	2,723	2,880	3,165	3,430	3,634	3,815
Deficit or surplus	-401	-480	-341	-225	-203	-197	-169	-145	-9	160	211	251
Adjusted baseline[a]												
Defense	407	452	475	489	502	522	541	559	584	595	621	649
Appropriated spending	419	448	464	475	491	507	523	541	559	578	598	617
Mandatory spending	1,188	1,257	1,299	1,366	1,439	1,525	1,616	1,715	1,829	1,910	2,048	2,174
Subtotal: spending excluding interest	2,014	2,157	2,238	2,330	2,432	2,554	2,680	2,815	2,972	3,083	3,267	3,440
Net interest	157	155	185	229	277	318	354	384	414	447	478	514
Total spending	2,171	2,312	2,423	2,559	2,709	2,872	3,034	3,199	3,386	3,530	3,745	3,954
Revenue	1,770	1,821	1,988	2,129	2,260	2,393	2,535	2,678	2,810	2,949	3,119	3,267
Deficit or surplus	-401	-491	-435	-430	-449	-479	-499	-521	-576	-581	-626	-687

Source: Congressional Budget Office, "The Budget and Economic Outlook: An Update," August 2003; Brookings-Urban Tax Policy Center; authors' calculations.

a. These numbers include CBO estimates for discretionary spending that have been inflated for population growth and CBO estimates for mandatory spending that have been increased for Medicare reforms, including the drug prescription benefits. Revenues are based on the Tax Policy Center model, assuming an extension of the 2001, 2002, and 2003 tax cuts beyond 2010 and assuming an amendment to the alternative minimum tax. See text for more details.

Although the CBO's economic projections are reasonable, its budget projections are distorted by congressional rules. The CBO is required to assume that whatever current law requires will actually happen. For example, CBO projections assume that long-standing provisions of the tax code, such as the research and development tax credit, expire and are not extended. If these provisions were to expire, the deficit would be smaller, but Congress is unlikely to allow them to do so. More important, the CBO projections assume—because the law says so—that tax cuts enacted in 2001 expire at the end of 2010 and all tax rates return to their pre-2001 levels. For example, the estate tax would be fully phased out in 2010 and then be reinstated in 2011. The additional tax cuts enacted in 2002 and 2003 also expire within the ten-year window. Congress is likely to correct this erratic policy. Indeed, President George W. Bush has asked that the new tax provisions be made permanent. The projections also assume that increasing numbers of taxpayers—as many as 33 million in 2010, compared with roughly 2.4 million today—pay the alternative minimum tax (AMT), although Congress is almost certain to amend the law to reduce the number of AMT payers substantially. Moreover, the CBO projections assume that discretionary spending—the money that Congress appropriates on an annual basis—increases only enough to keep up with inflation, even though the population is growing.

To give a more realistic picture of how both spending and revenues might grow over the next ten years, we have altered the assumptions in the following ways and extended the projections for one more year, to fiscal year 2014 (figure 1-4 and table 1-1).

We assume that

—discretionary spending increases in line with population growth as well as inflation; that is, we assume that real discretionary spending per person is held constant;

—Congress will extend temporary tax provisions now on the books and make the 2001, 2002, and 2003 tax changes permanent; and

— Congress will restrict the growth of the number of taxpayers subject to the alternative minimum tax.

We also add the cost of the prescription drug benefit and other changes in Medicare enacted at the end of the first session of this Congress.

Figure 1-4. *Baseline and Adjusted Outcomes as Percent of GDP, 2003–14*
Percent of GDP

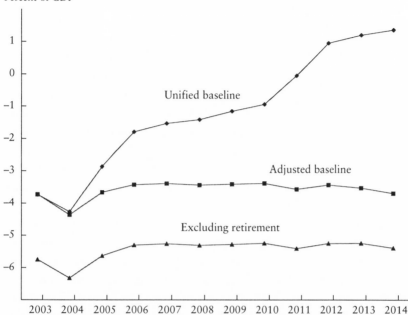

Source: Authors' calculations and Congressional Budget Office, "The Budget and Economic Outlook: An Update," August 2003.

These adjustments transform the deficit outlook. Instead, of moving toward balance over the decade, the deficit averages more than 3 percent of GDP over the ten-year period and remains at $687 billion in 2014. Moreover, the major retirement programs (Social Security, Medicare, and the government's own programs for federal employees) run substantial cash surpluses in this period. If these surpluses are excluded, the annual deficits average more than 5 percent of GDP and reach more than $1 trillion in 2014.

Deficits beyond 2014

Although the deficits expected over the coming ten years are very large, they pale beside those projected in subsequent decades if policies are not changed. As the generation born after World War II retires, longevity continues to increase, and medical costs keep rising, federal spending for retirement programs will accelerate rapidly. The CBO projects that if benefits are not changed, spending for Social Security will rise from 4.2 percent of GDP in 2010 to 5.9 percent by 2030 and 6.2 percent by 2050.[5] Even if medical care costs rise only 1 percent faster than per capita GDP—an optimistic assumption in view of recent increases—expenditures for Medicare and Medicaid would rise from 4.8 percent of GDP in 2010 to 8.4 percent in 2030 to 11.5 percent in 2050. Unless Americans are willing to shoulder a continuously rising tax burden, they must find ways to reduce these exploding costs before rising debt and interest costs engulf the budget and sap the economy's strength.

Why Deficits Matter

Unless the public is convinced that deficits matter, and matter quite a lot, political leaders have little incentive to do much about them. They may talk about the need for fiscal discipline and even propose small measures that move the federal budget in that direction, but serious deficit reduction is not likely to be a winning political strategy.

Democrats have learned that hair-shirt policies don't win them any friends and may even backfire. The Clinton administration spent eight years trying to bring the deficits it inherited under control, only to see the surpluses that emerged at the end of their time in office used to finance a large tax cut that primarily benefited a Republican constituency. Republicans, for their part, have gone from being the party of fiscal discipline to the party that sees deficits as a useful tool for constraining federal spending and shrinking government. The public, in the meantime, is confused. People hear in one speech that deficit-producing tax cuts are exactly what we need to produce jobs and growth and in another that tax cuts are a risky strategy that ultimately reduces standards of living. They are no longer sure what to believe. The problem is that deficits may be good when the economy is operating below its capacity, with a lot of unemployment, but bad once it has recovered. For countries, as for families, borrowing to meet emergencies is different from borrowing on a sustained basis to live beyond one's means. As President Bush has noted, deficits during wartime or recession may be entirely appropriate. For this reason, current deficits are beneficial in the short run because they are stimulating the economy and putting people back to work. Very little of the rising debt burden projected over the next decade, however, is related to temporary economic stimulus or short-run emergencies such as the war in Iraq. These deficits will persist for the foreseeable future, because spending is projected to grow faster than revenue.

So just how bad are deficits, and how can the long-term damage they create be better communicated to the public? Here we consider five arguments in favor of greater fiscal responsibility.

EFFECTS ON LONG-TERM GROWTH. Our colleague Charles Schultze once likened deficits not to the wolf at the door, but to termites in the woodwork. By this he meant that deficits gradually weaken the ability of workers to produce goods and services, thereby constraining wage increases and the growth of family incomes. Wage increases depend on how fast worker productivity grows. A major key to productivity growth, in turn, is investment in expanded business facilities and know-how—everything from robotics on the factory floor to a computer on every desk.[6] But when governments run deficits, they must compete with businesses for scarce financial capital, driving up its cost or reducing its availability to the private sector.[7] Just how much damage currently projected deficits will do depends on several assumptions, such as how much money we are able to borrow from abroad. But a conservative estimate is that a $5.3 trillion accumulation of additional debt over the next ten years would reduce national income by $212 billion annually at the end of the period. This translates into about $1,800 less annual income for the average household than it otherwise would have earned.[8]

HOUSEHOLD FINANCE. Households will find it more difficult to borrow to buy a home, a car, or a college education for their children. Interest rates are likely to rise at least 1 percentage point, based on estimates from a variety of studies.[9] This translates into higher costs for most households. For example, monthly payments on a thirty-year fixed-rate mortgage of $250,000 rise from $1,500 to $1,663 when interest rates rise from 6 percent to 7 percent. Over the life of the loan, this household ends up paying about $2,000 a year in extra interest payments to the lender.[10] Some industries, such as housing, automobiles, furniture, and appliances will be more affected than others. In addition, younger households that are still buying and furnishing their homes are likely to be adversely affected, while retirees with substantial assets will gain by earning more on their fixed-income investments.

DEPENDENCE ON THE REST OF THE WORLD. When government borrowing is growing faster than American domestic saving, domestic investment will be squeezed *unless* Americans are able to borrow from other countries. In recent years foreigners have provided much of the capital that has enabled American productivity to rise. In 2002, foreigners purchased 58 percent of new Treasury debt.[11] But such borrowing is costly. To begin with, part of our future income will be owed to the citizens of other countries. Second, high rates of borrowing from abroad that increase our net indebtedness to the rest of the world create risks for the economy. We are now borrowing to the tune of half a trillion dollars a year.[12] One danger is that foreigners will lose confidence in the United States and stop sending us their money. The value of the dollar would then fall—indeed some decline has already occurred—and our living standards would suffer as we had to pay more, by way of increased exports, for the goods we buy from abroad. Although the fall of the dollar would likely be gradual, there is some chance of a precipitous drop, which could lead to a sharp interest rate spike and possibly trigger a recession. An even more pessimistic scenario would be a financial crisis similar to those experienced when investors lost confidence in Argentina, Mexico, or East Asia. Finally, this dependence on the rest of the world for inflows of capital is not only risky for the United States, but also bad for the rest of the world. It is ironic, and some would say immoral, that the wealthiest nation in the world is forced to borrow from other countries to maintain current consumption.[13]

DEBT-SERVICING COSTS. Interest obligations of the federal government are slated to grow from $155 billion in 2004 to $514 billion in 2014, or by $359 billion. These extra costs are the result of both rising interest rates and increased borrowing by the federal government. By 2014, more than one out of every five dollars collected in individual income taxes (or all of corporate income taxes collected) will be needed just to pay these *added* debt-servicing costs, leaving less revenue to pay for the other things that government provides.[14] For example, just the projected *increase* in annual interest payments between now and 2014 would be enough to finance more than half of all projected defense spending in that year.

IMPOSING A BURDEN ON FUTURE GENERATIONS. There is no way to avoid paying the costs of government forever. Lower taxes now mean higher taxes later on. Today's children and young adults and their descendants will have to pay the bill. Meanwhile, deficits are likely to put downward pressure on spending for education, nutrition, and health care that could make today's children more productive and thus better able to pay these future bills.

Can We Expect to Grow out of the Deficits?

Deficits are very sensitive to the rate of economic growth. Official CBO projections (and the adjusted baseline used in this volume) are based on the assumption that the economy will grow at an average annual real rate of 3 percent over the next decade.[15] This forecast reflects the effects the CBO expects recent tax cuts to have on both short- and long-term growth.

A faster or a slower rate of economic growth than the CBO (and most private forecasters) project could change the deficit picture materially. For example, a real growth rate of 4 percent rather than 3 percent would eliminate the deficit at the end of ten years.[16] On the other hand, a slower rate of growth than that forecast would have the opposite effect, ballooning deficits to much higher levels.

How likely are these alternative economic scenarios and the different deficit pictures they imply? First, it must be noted that all projections, including the CBO's, are often wrong. Second, projections have as frequently been too optimistic as too pessimistic. Finally, although the economy has often averaged much more than 3 percent real growth for a quarter or even for a year, it has done so over an entire decade only once since World War II—and that was during the 1960s, when the economy managed to survive the entire decade without suffering a downturn. The annual real growth rate during the decades of the 1970s, 1980s, and 1990s averaged close to 3 percent.

Many people believe that recent tax cuts may encourage more work, more saving, and more investment by increasing the after-tax return for such activities. At the same time, tax cuts may make some people feel wealthier than they were before and, as a result, may cause them to work, save, and invest less. Finally, tax cuts that are deficit financed absorb savings by households and businesses that could otherwise go into private investment and thus tend to affect economic growth adversely.

Most studies, including those done by scholars, by the CBO, and by the congressional Joint Committee on Taxation, find that the net effects of recent tax cuts on longer-term economic growth are negligible. For example, the CBO concludes that "the revenue measures enacted since 2001 will boost labor supply by between 0.4 and 0.6 percent from 2004 to 2008 and up to 0.2 percent in 2009 to 2013 . . . but the tax legislation will probably have a negative effect on saving, investment, and capital accumulation over the next 10 years. . . . The tax laws' net effect on potential output . . . will probably be negative in the second five years."[17]

The effects of tax cuts might be more positive if more of the revenue loss were offset by cutting back other spending or raising other revenues. As it is, it's hard to escape the conclusion that recent tax cuts have done little if anything to improve the nation's long-term growth prospects and may have harmed them. What is needed to enhance long-term growth is higher national saving—not the lower saving generated by bigger deficits.

Of course, economic growth rates are quite unpredictable. U.S. growth might turn out to be higher than expected for any number of reasons. If that should happen, taking actions now to make sharp reductions in the budget deficit would still be good policy. The chances that we would somehow "overdo" deficit reduction are tiny to begin with, particularly when we take into account that ten years from now, even with substantially higher growth, the budget deficit excluding the government retirement programs will still be very large. Politically, measures strong enough to slash the deficit radically, while devilishly difficult to enact, are easy to undo. In the unlikely event that deficit reduction threatens to go too far, removing the threat will be no problem. But a mistake in the opposite direction will get harder to correct the longer deficits persist.

Deficit Goals and Policy Choices

Almost no one thinks that the currently projected deficits are a good thing. But there is disagreement about how much priority should be given to reducing them and what our deficit reduction goals should be.

A limited objective would be to reduce deficits to 1 percent or 2 percent of GDP on the grounds that the nation has lived with deficits of this size in the past and could survive living with them in the future. A more ambitious goal would be to eliminate the deficit, excluding the trust funds for Social Security, Medicare, and government pensions. These programs have their own dedicated revenues and are now producing large cashflow surpluses that are masking the size of the deficit in the rest of the government. These retirement program surpluses, however, will soon begin to disappear, so it seems shortsighted to allow them to hide the true magnitude of the deficits that will confront us in the future. The deficit projected for 2014, excluding the retirement accounts, is just over $1 trillion.

In this volume, we take a middle ground and focus on reducing the deficit in the unified budget to zero over a ten-year period. Even this relatively modest goal will require difficult choices and strong political will. The budget deficit problem cannot be solved in the abstract. It will require choosing to take specific actions that have political risks. The purpose of the next chapter is to give concrete illustrations of the type of spending cuts or tax increases that would be required to achieve budget balance in a decade. We hope these illustrations will give the reader a sense of the magnitude of the policy changes that would be required to balance the budget and stimulate serious discussion of different ways of doing so.

Notes

1. Congressional Budget Office, "The Budget and Economic Outlook: An Update," August 2003, pp. 4–10.

2. Richard W. Stevenson and Edmund L. Andrews, "No Escaping the Red Ink as Bush Pens '04 Agenda," *New York Times*, November 29, 2003, p. A10.

3. William G. Gale and Peter R. Orszag, "The Budget Outlook: Analysis and Implications," *Tax Notes*, October 6, 2003, pp. 145–57.

4. Gale and Orszag, "The Budget Outlook."

5. U.S. Congressional Budget Office, *The Long-Term Budget Outlook* (December 2003).

6. Council of Economic Advisers, "Economic Report of the President," February 2003.

7. Increased saving by Americans (in response to higher interest rates or in anticipation of the need to pay higher taxes in the future) or borrowing from abroad can cushion this effect. But more saving requires that people reduce their consumption now, and more borrowing requires that they earmark more of their future incomes to compensate foreigners for financing our investment.

8. Based on same method as on p. 147 of Gale and Orszag, "The Budget Outlook." National savings reduced by two-thirds of $5.3 trillion = $3.53 trillion. $3.53 × .06 = $212 billion. $212 billion/119 million households = $1,782 per household in 2014.

9. William G. Gale and Peter R. Orszag, "The Economic Effects of Sustained Budget Deficits," *National Tax Journal,* September 2003. Deficits equal to 3 percent of GDP would raise interest rates by between 60 and 180 basis points, with a mean of 120.

10 See www.interest.com for mortgage calculators.

11. Gale and Orszag, "The Budget Outlook," p. 153.

12. See www.bea.gov. The U.S. current account deficit was $278.1 billion for the first half of 2003.

13. Kenneth Rogoff, "The Debtor's Empire," *Washington Post,* October 20, 2003, p. A.23.

14. Personal income taxes will be around $1.6 trillion in 2014. $359 billion in interest obligations is 22.4 percent of these taxes.

15. Congressional Budget Office, "The Budget and Economic Outlook," p. 43.

16. Gale and Orszag, "The Budget Outlook," p. 153.

17. Congressional Budget Office, "The Budget and Economic Outlook," p. 45.

2

Getting to Balance:
Three Alternative Plans

RON HASKINS, ALICE M. RIVLIN, AND
ISABEL SAWHILL

When a budget is in deficit there are only two ways—other than faster growth in the economy—to bring it into balance. Spending must be cut or revenue increased. Both are difficult to achieve politically and sure to cause pain. After all, deficits do not happen accidentally. Spending programs are enacted because a majority in Congress deems the activities they support to be necessary or at least desirable. Beneficiaries of federal spending—whether they receive Medicare or a contract to build Navy airplanes or work in a local Head Start program—are sure to oppose cuts in their particular program. Moreover, they are likely to be more vocal than those who might benefit marginally from the corresponding cut in the deficit. Similarly, tax increases are certain to be unpopular. Even if the group whose taxes are raised is small, its members will argue strongly that the increase is damaging and unfair, while the larger group that stands to benefit from deficit reduction is unlikely to express support for the increase.

In this chapter we illustrate three plans for reaching balance in the unified budget over the next decade—plans that differ in the ways they

Table 2-1. *Illustrative Changes in 2014 by Plan Type*
Billions of dollars

Item	Smaller government plan	Larger government plan	Better government plan
Total deficit reduction	687	687	687
Interest payment reduction	–153	–153	–153
Tax increase	134	629	401
Programmatic spending net change	–400	95	–134
Defense net change	0	–60	–60
Increase	0	0	0
Decrease	0	–60	–60
Non-defense net change	–400	155	–74
Increase	0	185	41
Decrease	–400	–30	–115

Source: Authors' calculations and Congressional Budget Office, "The Budget and Economic Outlook: An Update," August 2003.

mix spending cuts and revenue increases to get to balance (table 2-1). For convenience we call them the smaller government plan, the larger government plan, and the better government plan. All three plans start from the adjusted baseline projections described in chapter 1. These projections indicate that in the absence of policy change, the deficit in 2014 will be about $687 billion. Balancing the unified budget by that year will produce interest savings of around $153 billion, leaving a deficit of $534 billion to be eliminated by spending reductions or revenue increases. Choosing the more stringent criterion of balancing the budget excluding the federal retirement programs necessitates additional deficit reduction of $316 billion. As the plans amply illustrate, even meeting the less ambitious target requires tough choices that are sure to be unpopular.

Our three plans reflect three contrasting views about the role of the federal government. The smaller government plan emphasizes spending reduction and is likely to appeal to people who believe that

—the federal government is too big and has taken on too many responsibilities;

—with the exception of national security, the objectives of many federal programs could be attained more effectively by states, localities, or private organizations and individuals;

—the economy would operate more productively if the federal government were smaller and less intrusive.

The larger government plan, by contrast, emphasizes revenue increases and cuts in defense spending to fund existing domestic programs and new initiatives. It will appeal to those who believe that

—most domestic programs of the federal government should be continued;

—new initiatives should be added to achieve such goals as helping low-income people, preserving the environment, or improving education;

—taxes must be raised to fund a more activist government in a fiscally responsible way.

The better government plan is likely to appeal to those who believe that

—government performance could be improved by reducing less effective programs to make room for higher-priority activities such as making work more attractive and rewarding to low-income people, increasing health care coverage, supporting the states in improving education, and preserving the environment;

—these objectives should be met without increasing the size of government and with as much reliance on market forces as possible.

The plan involves a restructuring of both defense and non-defense spending. To achieve balance in 2014 it relies on a modest net spending reduction combined with tax increases to restore revenues to their historic share of GDP.

The Smaller Government Plan

This plan achieves balance over ten years by cutting $400 billion (about 75 percent of the projected deficit minus interest savings) from projected domestic spending in 2014. It also includes revenue increases of $134 billion (about 25 percent of the projected deficit), achieved without changing either tax rates or tax brackets (table 2-2). The smaller government plan would reduce total spending as a share of GDP from 20.2 percent in 2003 to 18.3 percent in 2014. That might sound like a modest reduction. But rising wages and prices, especially the price of medical care, tend to increase the cost of government faster than the economy grows, while beneficiaries of retirement programs are increasing. Hence, quite drastic

Table 2-2. *A Smaller Government Plan to Balance the Budget in 2014, Primarily by Cutting Spending*

Item	Billions of dollars
Total deficit reduction	687
Minus debt service savings	−153
Subtotal: tax increases and spending cuts to eliminate deficit	534
Plus funding for new initiatives	0
Total: tax increases and spending cuts to eliminate deficit	534
Changes in the budget	
Revenue change	134
Spending cuts	−400
Commercial subsidies	−138
Devolution	−123
Wasteful spending	−7
Non-defense discretionary	−58
Entitlement	−74

Source: Authors' calculations and Congressional Budget Office, "The Budget and Economic Outlook: An Update," August 2003. Note that sums do not add to totals because of rounding.

program cuts are required to reduce government's share of GDP by even 1 percentage point.

The programs reduced or eliminated in the smaller government plan have passionate defenders and strong political support. That is why they were enacted and have remained in the budget. Indeed, putting together a deficit reduction plan that relies heavily on spending cuts illustrates the political difficulty—some would say impossibility—of achieving balance this way. But unless political leaders are prepared to take unpopular actions on either the spending or the revenue side of the budget or both, fiscal responsibility will not be restored. Politicians who talk vaguely of "reducing big government" must get specific about the programs that must be cut if their approach is to be taken seriously.

Over much of the past century, the federal government enacted thousands of new spending programs. Some no longer have a persuasive rationale. Maybe they were enacted to shield an industry whose protection can no longer be justified. Maybe they were undertaken to encourage state or local governments to pay attention to problems they were neglecting or groups they were not serving. Now, however, these programs have ardent defenders, and the need for federal funding has diminished. Moreover, the plethora of federal grants and mandates, with their onerous and some-times conflicting requirements, impedes the effective execution of legiti-mate state and local government functions. Still other programs may simply be ineffective, wasteful, or badly managed. The smaller govern-ment plan illustrates how the federal budget might be balanced by weed-ing out inappropriate, obsolete, and low-priority federal activities.

Reducing Commercial Subsidies

Public subsidies to commercial activities, while sometimes justified by temporary emergencies, tend to postpone needed adjustments to eco-nomic and technological change and lead to misallocation of capital and ultimately to a lower standard of living. If public subsidies to commercial activities were eliminated from the federal budget, the deficit would decline and economic growth would likely increase.

Examples of commercial subsidy programs that could be eliminated or privatized—meaning that service would continue but fees would cover the costs—abound. In 2001 the Cato Institute drew up a list of eighty such programs.[1] Eliminating or privatizing those eighty programs would save a total of about $137.5 billion in 2014 (see table 2-3 for an illustra-tive list). The commercial subsidies take a variety of forms. For example, the Export-Import Bank provides subsidized services to American com-panies that do business outside the United States. These activities are of questionable value and in any case should be paid for by the businesses that use them. Eliminating this bank would save $2.7 billion in 2014. The Energy Department subsidizes applied research for fossil fuels although energy markets provide ample incentives for companies to develop new ways to find fossil fuels and bring them to market. About $0.7 billion could be saved in 2014 by eliminating the fossil fuels pro-gram. Similarly, the Federal Aviation Administration provides grants to large and medium-sized hub airports to expand runways, improve secu-rity, and make other capital improvements when it would be far more effi-cient to pay for these activities through user fees charged to the airplanes and passengers who use the facilities. Terminating this program would save $3.4 billion in 2014.

Table 2-3. *The Smaller Government Plan: Illustrative Cuts in Commercial Subsidies*
Billions of dollars

Item	Cut in 2014
Export-Import Bank	2.7
Energy Department applied research for fossil fuels	0.7
Airport improvement program	3.4
Agriculture commodity price supports	23.0
Department of Energy science and research	4.7
Community Development Block Grants	8.0
Air traffic control	10.4
Agency for International Development	3.8
Total cuts in Cato proposal[a]	137.5

Source: Stephen Slivinski, "The Corporate Welfare Budget: Bigger Than Ever," Cato Institute Policy Analysis 415 (Washington, October 10, 2001), table 1.
a. This list is illustrative of the total $137.5 billion in possible cuts. Our estimate is based on adjusting the total savings of the Cato cuts by our inflation and population adjuster.

Returning Functions to the States

In the 1930s, Congress began setting up agencies and programs to carry out activities such as health care, housing, education, and transportation that had hitherto been state responsibilities. Hundreds of "categorical grants" influenced state and local spending priorities by providing federal funds to be spent in conformance with strict guidelines, often accompanied by the requirement that the state or local jurisdiction come up with money to match the federal contribution.

The explosion of federal categorical grants arguably led to excessive paperwork; overlapping, conflicting, and inappropriate federal requirements; and wasteful, ineffective spending. Presidents Nixon and Reagan both tried to clarify the responsibilities of the different levels of government and combine categorical grants into block grants to give states more flexibility. Neither appreciably reduced either the blizzard of grant programs or the confusion of responsibilities.

Eliminating federal spending for a range of activities more appropriate to state and local governments would help reduce the federal deficit. It would also encourage citizens to hold their state and local governments accountable for performing these functions without turning to the federal government for help. State and local dollars would no longer flow through the costly federal bureaucracy before returning to state and local governments in the form of grants. State and local governments would also be relieved of the costs of conforming to federal requirements. Services might also improve, because responsibility for delivering them would rest with governments that are more in touch with what citizens need than Washington is.

The smaller government plan would eliminate all federal discretionary spending for elementary and secondary education, housing and urban development, manpower training and related programs, environmental protection, and law enforcement. Eliminating Department of Education programs for elementary and secondary education would save $55.6 billion in 2014. Eliminating all discretionary spending programs in the Department of Housing and Urban Development would save another $42.4 billion in 2014. Eliminating Labor Department spending for training and employment services, Employment Service/one-stops, community service for older Americans, veterans training, and disability programs would save $9.9 billion. Cutting all Environmental Protection Agency spending for clean water, drinking water, brownfields, targeted water infrastructure, Superfund, and related programs would save another $11.2 billion. And eliminating Justice Department spending for state and local law enforcement assistance would save $3.9 billion.

Devolving all these activities to the states and their localities would reduce federal spending in 2014 by $123 billion (table 2-4). It would radically reduce the role of the federal government in aiding states and localities and pass the deficit down to lower levels of government already struggling to maintain budget balance. States and localities would have to decide whether to continue the services no longer supported by the federal government, and if so, how to pay for them. Lower federal taxes would make it somewhat easier for states and localities to raise revenue. Poorer states would be harder hit than wealthier ones because federal grants tend to compensate for interstate inequalities in resources. Some would argue for replacing the categorical grants with a new program of federal revenue sharing for general purposes distributed on the basis of a formula that would favor poorer states. We have not included such a program here because doing so would offset much of the deficit reduction that spending cuts promise.

Table 2-4. *The Smaller Government Plan: Cuts through Devolution*
Billions of dollars

Item	Cut in 2014
Elementary, secondary, and other education	55.6
Housing programs	42.4
Manpower training programs	9.9
Environmental Protection Agency programs	11.2
Justice: state and local	3.9
Total	123.0

Source: Executive Office of the President, *Budget of the U.S. Government: Fiscal Year 2004* (February 2003).

Reducing Wasteful Spending

The 2003 congressional budget resolution required the General Accounting Office and all authorizing committees of the House of Representatives to identify waste, fraud, and abuse in mandatory spending programs within their jurisdictions. The GAO and the committees were then required to summarize their findings in a written report to the House Budget Committee. On October 2, 2003, committee chairman Jim Nussle released a report summarizing the findings from these reports.[2] Most of the major savings proposals uncovered by this exercise are listed in table 2-5. The total savings, most of which were based on estimates either by CBO or by GAO, is $7 billion in 2014.

Of course, one person's waste is another person's absolutely necessary spending. Few of these proposals for savings would be politically popular; indeed, if there were no resistance to making these cuts, they would have been made long ago. But if Congress were under pressure to reduce spending, most of these proposals would be less painful than other cuts in the smaller government plan.

Additional Cuts in Non-Defense Discretionary Spending

Rapid increases in discretionary spending, which amounted to nearly 40 percent of total federal spending in 2003, illustrate the absence of federal budget discipline in recent years. In the six years between 1994 and 1999, discretionary spending rose about 1 percent a year on average, and in 1996 it declined. During four of those years, defense spending fell, with

Table 2-5. *The Smaller Government Plan: Cuts in Wasteful Spending*
Billions of dollars

Item	Cut in 2014
Competitive bidding in Medicare	1.0
Reduce overpayments in Supplemental Security Income program	2.0
Reduce overpayments in Unemployment Compensation program	2.0
Require states to comparison shop for Medicaid drugs	2.0
Total	7.0

Source: House Budget Committee, "Sampling of Waste, Fraud, and Abuse from Committee, GAO Submissions," October 2, 2003 (press release).

the average for the period of –1 percent. But even non-defense discretionary spending increased by an average of only around 3 percent. By contrast, the five years between 2000 and 2004 have seen explosive growth—averaging 9.5 percent a year—in discretionary spending, according to the CBO. Defense led the way, with average increases of 10.5 percent, but non-defense discretionary spending also rose rapidly, with yearly increases averaging well over 8.5 percent and reaching an amazing 12 percent in 2002. Increased spending on homeland security after the attacks of September 11, 2001, undoubtedly played an important role in this remarkable rise in discretionary spending. Even so, this brief review of the budget figures shows that offsetting cuts in other spending categories were few and negligible. In other words, our policy is now not just simultaneous increases in spending on guns and butter, but increases in spending on homeland security as well.

Most of the programs eliminated in the smaller government plan for commercial subsidies and all the programs ended under the devolution proposals are domestic discretionary programs. Three additional cuts in domestic discretionary spending are listed in table 2-6. These include terminating the National Aeronautic and Space Administration's program of manned flight, ending earmarks for local projects in the highway construction program, and slowing the rate of growth of the National Institutes of Health. The combined savings from these three cuts is $22.9 billion in 2014.

According to our adjusted baseline projections for non-defense discretionary spending (based on the assumption that annual growth over the next decade will equal inflation plus population growth), such spending

Table 2-6. *The Smaller Government Plan: Cuts in Non-Defense Discretionary Spending*
Billions of dollars

Item	Cut in 2014
Reduced National Aeronautics and Space Administration	9.0
Highway earmarks for local projects	1.9
Slow growth of National Institutes of Health (2 percent in real terms)	12.0
Cap on remaining discretionary spending	35.5
Total	58.4

will increase by an average of less than 3.6 percent a year. Given the annual average increase of more than 8.5 percent in recent years, even achieving 3.6 percent would be remarkable. Nonetheless, in an effort to balance the budget by holding down the size of government, a more stringent cap would be plausible. Imposing a 2.5 percent annual cap on nominal growth in non-defense discretionary spending would force hard choices. If growth were allowed in a few programs, others would have to grow at less than the rate of inflation, some would be cut in nominal dollars, and some might be terminated. The saving in 2014 from the 2.5 percent cap against the baseline that remains after the other cuts in discretionary spending is $35.5 billion (table 2-6).

Reducing Entitlement Spending

Politicians and voters are understandably reluctant to cut Social Security, Medicare, or Medicaid benefits, because elderly, disabled, and low-income people depend heavily on these programs. Moreover, it seems unfair to cut benefits for current retirees—or those eligible to retire in the near future—who have planned their retirement on the expectation of receiving these benefits. Nevertheless, although few elected officials are willing to say so, retirement programs must be modified to avoid their consuming the entire federal budget. Over the next thirty years, as more and more baby boomers retire, longevity continues to increase, and medical costs rise, the liabilities of Social Security, Medicare, and Medicaid will explode. If the current budget problem is a gale, the long-term problem is a hurricane.

Table 2-7. *The Smaller Government Plan: Cuts in Entitlements*
Billions of dollars

Item	Cut in 2014
Medicaid	
Reduce enhanced match for administration	2.0
Reduce spending for Medicaid administration	4.5
Social Security	
Raise retirement age starting in 2012	1.4
Consumer price index adjustment: benefits	17.0
Medicare	
Indirect teaching payments	5.0
Reduce direct payments for medical education	1.1
Premium increase in supplemental medical insurance	16.0
Payments to managed care	5.0
Convert Graduate Medicare Education to block grant	2.0
Convert DSH payments to block grant	3.0
Partially reduce prospective payment system update factor	4.1
Simplify cost sharing	2.0
Reduce payments to home health care	3.5
Reduce copayments on home health episodes	1.5
Other programs	
Voucher for federal employees' health benefit	3.9
Limit cost-of-living adjustment for federal employees	2.0
Total	74.0

Sources: Henry J. Aaron and Peter R. Orszag, chapter 5 of this volume, and Congressional Budget Office, *Budget Options* (March 2003).

Because of the importance of advance notice, proposals to constrain spending for the retirement programs do not generate large budget savings in the near term, so it is tempting to postpone them. Delaying the reductions, however, just makes the necessary changes larger. The smaller government plan contains a list of reductions in entitlement benefits (primarily in Social Security, Medicare, and Medicaid) that contribute roughly $74 billion to budget balance in 2014 and generate much larger savings in the years that follow (see table 2-7). Several of these proposals are described in chapter 5; the rest are to be found in the CBO publication *Budget Options*.[3]

The reform that would save the most involves revising the way Social Security benefits are adjusted for inflation. As explained in more detail in chapter 5, the Census Bureau has known for many years that the consumer price index (CPI), which is now used to adjust Social Security benefits each year, overstates growth in the cost of living. Substituting a more accurate index developed by the Bureau of Labor Statistics would reduce Social Security spending in 2014 by $17 billion, while fully protecting the elderly against inflation. If the new index were also applied to the personal exemption, the standard deduction, and the income levels that define tax brackets, another $18 billion could be saved in 2014 through increased income taxes and reduced spending in a few additional programs (these latter savings are listed in table 2-8 as revenue increases).

An additional $16 billion could be saved in 2014 by reducing the federal subsidy for supplemental medical insurance (SMI) premiums for most Medicare enrollees. When Medicare was enacted in 1965, the SMI premium was set to cover half of program costs, but the share of costs covered by premiums has declined over the years to 25 percent. Under the proposal discussed in chapter 5, the fee would gradually be raised to a minimum of 35 percent of cost for Medicare enrollees other than those with low incomes, rising to 80 percent for couples with incomes greater than $400,000.

Another major savings proposal, discussed in detail in the CBO volume *Budget Options*, would decrease Medicare payments to hospitals through the prospective payment system. Savings of more than $4.1 billion can be produced in 2014 by slightly reducing the update factor, a policy justified by the substantial profit that hospitals make on the average Medicare recipient who receives inpatient care.

These and the other savings proposals outlined in our tables achieve our goal of $400 billion in 2014. These cuts involve drastic changes in what the federal government does and its relation to the state, local, and private sectors. Whether the political system could adopt these changes—or even a substantial portion of them—depends heavily on whether the Republican Party returns to its historic goal of reducing the size of government.

Under normal circumstances, cuts as large as those proposed in the smaller government plan would be deemed impossible. But circumstances are not normal. Action must be taken to control unsustainable deficits. If spending cuts are to dominate the antideficit action, Republicans, both because they control Congress and the presidency and because their tax cuts contribute importantly to future deficits, will have to lead the way. The spending cuts in the smaller government plan are not the only possible cuts, but they illustrate the magnitude of the challenge.

Revenue Increases

The spending cuts illustrated above are drastic, but still they do not generate enough savings to balance even the unified budget in 2014—not to mention the budget excluding retirement program surpluses. The authors have therefore resorted to revenue increases to achieve balance, even though advocates of smaller government generally oppose any tax increases.

In recent years, tax cutting (especially reducing income tax rates) appears to have become more important to Republicans than balancing the budget, so most tax increases would likely be opposed by most Republicans in Congress as well as by the Bush administration. Nevertheless, only a few years ago Republicans were vehement about the importance of a balanced federal budget. Indeed, they felt so strongly about it that they sponsored, and came within a few votes of passing, legislation to amend the Constitution to require Congress to balance the federal budget each year. If the consequences of large deficits were to create pressure to balance the budget, some Republicans might recapture the budget-balance fervor of the 1990s and support modest revenue increases as part of a package that depends primarily on spending cuts.

To maximize appeal to advocates of smaller government, this package avoids two kinds of tax increases. It includes no changes in the tax rates or tax brackets enacted in the tax legislation of 2001 and 2003. Nor does it change the capital gains tax, which was also modified in 2003. Few elected Republicans would support such changes. Moreover, low tax rates increase economic activity and are consistent with the Republican philosophy of small government.

A set of tax code changes consistent with these criteria is shown in table 2-8. Six have modest revenue effect, but the other four produce significant additional revenue in 2014. The first would raise the federal tax on motor fuels by 12 cents a gallon, bringing the total federal tax to 30.4 cents a gallon for gas (36.4 cents a gallon for diesel fuel). In addition to raising more

Table 2-8. *The Smaller Government Plan: Revenue Increases*
Billions of dollars

Item	Cut in 2014
Tax credit for exclusion of interest income on state and local debt	2.0
Include employer-paid life insurance in taxable income	2.0
Include in adjusted gross income all income earned abroad by U.S. citizens	5.0
Eliminate some rules for inventory sales	7.0
Increase excise tax on cigarettes by 50 cents	7.0
Increase alcohol tax to $16 per proof gallon	6.0
Increase tax on motor fuel by 12 cents a gallon	20.0
Freeze estate tax at 2009 level	30.0
Consumer price index adjustment	18.0
Improve enforcement	37.0
Total	134.0

Sources: Henry J. Aaron and Peter R. Orszag, chapter 5 in this volume, and Congressional Budget Office, *Budget Options* (March 2003).

than $20 billion in 2014, these increases in the cost of motor fuel would decrease fuel consumption, reduce pollution and traffic congestion, and persuade some Americans to purchase more fuel-efficient cars and trucks. They would also, however, increase trucking and other transportation costs, contributing to higher prices for many goods and services. And the price increases would fall disproportionately on lower-income consumers.

A second substantial increase in revenue could be achieved by partially reversing the estate tax changes enacted in the tax legislation of 2001. As discussed in more detail in chapter 6 (see table 6-2), estates are taxed based on the value of assets transferred at death. The 2001 tax law reduced the estate tax by raising the amount of estate value exempted from the tax. The amount exempted was set at $1 million for 2002 and then gradually increased until it reached $3.5 million in 2009. The 2001 tax act also decreased the estate tax rate from a maximum of 55 percent to 45 percent. In 2010, the entire tax would be repealed. Retaining the 2009 version of the tax and dropping the tax rate to 35 percent would still greatly reduce the estate tax from its 2001 level, and only about 10,000 estates would pay the tax. Yet federal revenues would increase by about $30 billion in 2014. Ironically, the biggest revenue producer in our plan, worth $37 billion in 2014, is simply to give the Internal Revenue Service the resources it needs to enforce the tax laws we already have (see chapter 6 for details).

The Larger Government Plan

Many people find unpalatable the kind of retrenchment required by the smaller government option. Indeed, they argue that the federal government should be doing more not less than it now is to address various national problems. They point to the many citizens who lack health insurance, to the schools that fail to educate children, to global warming and other environmental problems that are not being adequately addressed. They argue that too many children are growing up in poverty and too many adults are out of work or earning too little to support a family. They emphasize that the distribution of income in the United States is not only less equal than it is in other advanced countries but that the gap between rich and poor has widened in recent decades and been exacerbated by recent tax cuts that have favored the affluent over the middle class or the poor. They believe that U.S. military strength needs to be supplemented by efforts to address world poverty, disease, and lack of literacy and by greater sharing of the military burden with our allies.

Those who favor a more robust federal role note that the private sector has no incentive to address the above-mentioned problems. State and local governments could, in principle, pick up some additional responsibilities but lack the fiscal capacity to do so and will face greater demands on their limited resources as baby boomers increase Medicaid costs that have been rising at double-digit rates for more than a decade. Furthermore, states are constrained in their ability to raise taxes by their need to remain competitive with other jurisdictions.

The issue is not just whether it is desirable to address some or all of these problems but also what the effects would be on the nation's economy, on the social fabric, and on the well-being of the average citizen. Unlike those who favor smaller government, advocates of a stronger federal role believe that it is possible to design effective programs to accomplish various social objectives without compromising growth or international competitiveness. They point to other advanced countries that have far larger public sectors and higher tax burdens than the United States, along with more public amenities, less inequality, and fewer social problems, and whose rates of growth and ability to compete have not been significantly affected as a result. While few argue that the United

States should adopt a European-style welfare state or that programs don't need to be carefully crafted to avoid unintended consequences, these advocates of a more activist government reject the idea that individual welfare could not be greatly improved through collective action.

This vision is not an entirely partisan affair. Many members of the public and their elected representatives from both parties share at least some of these concerns and want to see them addressed. Still, a natural place to look to see how an advocate of this point of view might address various social priorities and simultaneously deal with looming deficits is to review what the various candidates for the 2004 Democratic presidential nomination proposed during the primary season. Different candidates espoused different agendas, of course, but those agendas shared several common themes, including extending health care to more of those who now lack it; providing states with funds for homeland security, education, and infrastructure; providing access to higher education and to a preschool experience for the young; and preserving or enhancing Social Security and Medicare benefits for the elderly. On foreign policy, most candidates favored more sharing of costs with our allies to rebuild Iraq and more humanitarian assistance to poorer countries.

Because candidates who are specific about their plans open themselves to criticism of all sorts, they rarely offer sufficient detail to assess the cost of their agendas and their impact on long-term deficits. Still, it is instructive to look at the broad outlines of these Democratic campaign platforms and assess their effects on fiscal balance. As detailed below, the conclusion has to be that, whatever their other merits, none of the Democratic candidates' plans released during the primaries managed to close the fiscal gap and pay for proposed new initiatives. This is especially true of candidates who proposed to raise taxes only on the wealthy and not on the middle class as well. In fairness, it should be noted that they faced an incumbent president who had also failed to address the deficit and continued to argue for tax cuts that would produce still more red ink.

Several major Democratic candidates proposed a temporary stimulus package. Governor Howard Dean proposed a two-year $100 billion "Fund to Restore America" that would provide grants to the states for homeland security and infrastructure and thereby create more jobs. To some extent such spending would have effects on short-term economic growth similar to, if not greater than, the Bush administration's tax cuts and could thus be expected to produce more revenue as well. But it would also increase the deficits accumulated over the next decade and add to the burden of the debt.

The biggest split within Democratic ranks was between those who favor rolling back all the Bush tax cuts and those who want to eliminate only the cuts that went to the wealthiest Americans, generally those with more than $200,000 a year in income. This difference has major implications for the nation's ability to reduce longer-term deficits. Although scaling back tax cuts for the wealthy can provide resources to fund *some* new initiatives, these resources are far too small to fund *all* the new initiatives and also reduce the deficit.[4]

Some candidates tried to identify savings in other parts of the budget. Examples included investing in information technology to reduce health care costs (John Kerry) and reinstituting then–vice president Al Gore's National Performance Review to find savings by making government work better (Dean). But, not surprisingly, several candidates did not come up with a list of budget cuts to help pay for their top priorities. (Some discussed addressing corporate loopholes and avoidance in the tax system, which affect revenues, not spending.)

Health care was the "big spending" item in virtually every Democratic plan.[5] But other costly items included extending access to college and preschool for most if not all Americans.[6] Another big-ticket item, "fully funding" special education, would have provided significant relief to lower levels of government but would have cost the federal budget dearly (an estimated $225 billion over ten years).[7] In short, education would get substantial new resources in any liberal plan.

So what could an activist president and Congress do to fund some new priorities and yet head the country toward a balanced budget within a decade? Is it even possible to get there from here? And if so, what mix of new revenues and reduced spending would be required to free up sufficient resources both to fund some new priorities and to reduce the deficit?

Table 2-9 illustrates the possibilities. The larger governmental plan includes $185 billion in new spending and $629 billion in additional revenues. It achieves a balanced budget by 2014 by relying heavily on revenue increases. It would increase the share of total government spending

Table 2-9. *A Larger Government Plan to Balance the Budget in 2014, Primarily by Raising Revenue While Funding New Initiatives*

Item	Billions of dollars
Total deficit reduction	687
Minus debt service savings	–153
Subtotal	534
Plus funding for new initiatives	95
Total: tax increases and spending cuts to eliminate deficit	629
Changes in the budget	
Revenue change	629
Spending cuts	–90
Defense[a]	–60
Non-defense[b]	–30
New spending	185
Health[c]	100
Education[d]	60
Other[e]	25
Net increase in spending	95

Source: Authors' calculations; Congressional Budget Office, "The Budget and Economic Outlook: An Update," August 2003; Sara R. Collins, Karen Davis, and Jeanne M. Lambrew, "Health Care Reform Returns to the National Agenda: The 2004 Presidential Candidates' Proposals" (New York: Commonwealth Fund, September 2003, updated February 20, 2004). National Education Association, "IDEA Funding Coalition Offers Proposal" (www.nea.org/specialed/coalitionfunding2002.html); www.kucinich.us/index.php; Isabel Sawhill, "Investing in Children," Brookings Children's Roundtable Policy Brief 1 (April 1999).

a. Defense baseline includes spending in Iraq. These cuts assume a more peaceful world and less reconstruction by 2014.

b. For example, through a reinstated National Performance Review.

c. Kerry plan has $895 billion of spending over ten years.

d. Access to higher education through Pell grants, preschool, and more federal funding of special education.

e. Assistance to states, safety net programs, environment, international assistance especially for HIV/AIDS.

to 20.9 percent in 2014 from 20.2 percent in 2003. The spending included would pay for many of the proposed investments in health and education and would offer more modest amounts for assistance to the states, safety net programs, the environment, and humanitarian-oriented international assistance. We assume that some of these costs would be off-set by savings elsewhere in the budget. But even this assumption may be overly optimistic. Liberals are unlikely to want to cut existing programs deeply, and, as argued in chapter 3, opportunities to shift funds from defense to domestic spending are likely to be limited. The bulk of the resources needed to achieve fiscal stability and pay for new priorities would have to come from new revenues, whose possible sources are detailed in table 6-10. These revenues are derived from many tax measures, including scaling back the 2001 tax cuts that went to the affluent, raising payroll taxes for this same group, and creating a new value-added tax that would affect almost everyone.

It is worth noting here that we are assuming that the Bush tax cuts will be extended beyond their current expiration dates. If the cuts were not extended, much smaller revenue increases would be needed. But no one expects the tax cuts to "sunset." Any Democratic president elected in 2004 would find it politically difficult to raise taxes on the middle class and implement the other revenue changes contemplated here. If at least one house of Congress remained in Republican hands, the task would be much harder. Democrats would be forced either to scale back substantially their domestic promises, including perhaps their current commitment to maintain Social Security and Medicare benefits, or to live with large deficits indefinitely.

The Better Government Plan

The two plans just discussed—one that might be favored by advocates of small government and the other by those who think government isn't doing enough—illustrate the difficulty of closing the fiscal gap over the next decade and preparing for the baby boom's retirement. The first plan implies spending cuts that are unlikely to be approved, even if Republicans control the White House and both houses of Congress. The second envisions tax increases that are not likely to be politically feasible, even for a Democratic president and a more Democratic Congress.

But in addition to their political infeasibility, these two plans may miss the point. The issue should not be the size of government but its effectiveness. The better government plan is based on the view that government can be more effective without absorbing an increasing share of GDP. In that view, the goal of eliminating the deficit provides a powerful incentive to weed out ineffective and outmoded programs while meeting new objectives.

Unfortunately, not enough is known about the effectiveness of various government programs. And even where such information exists, reallocating resources in response to such evidence—or in response to changing national needs—is extremely difficult. The beneficiaries of existing programs, though sometimes relatively few in number, are usually knowledgeable and often organized to defend their programs. The general public is less well informed and has little ability or incentive to work toward scaling them back. Members of Congress and other political leaders know that staying in office requires being responsive to the specialized constituencies that benefit from particular programs, even at the cost of increasing the deficit. The result is that new programs are layered on top of old ones and budgetary resources are rarely reallocated to make government more effective. Analogous arguments can be made about tax cuts that favor particular groups at the expense of others and about persistent deficits that benefit the current generation at the expense of the next.

Budget rules that discipline the political process can help to correct these perverse political incentives and are discussed in the final section of this chapter. But in the end, rules are no substitute for making the hard choices. Table 2-10 sketches a third way of making those choices—the better government plan for balancing the budget in 2014 while funding a few limited new initiatives. That plan relies on revenue increases of $401 billion, spending cuts of $175 billion, and new spending of $41 billion. It would keep the share of total federal spending at about its current level relative to GDP (19.7 percent in 2014).

In the remainder of this volume the authors suggest what a restructured government that is no different in size from the present one might look like. The choices are difficult indeed. While the authors believe that the better government plan is both preferable to and more feasible than the other two, not all the authors agree with all components of the plan. Some of us think that defense spending needs to increase more or less than recommended in chapter 3. Some of us would provide more funding for the various domestic priorities, such as education and health care, discussed in chapter 4. Some of us think that more should be done sooner to curtail the growth of Social Security and Medicare discussed in chapter 5. And although we agree that revenues have to be an important part of the picture, we didn't try to forge a consensus on which parts of the tax system need to be modified. Still, we all believe that it is important to show

Table 2-10. *A Better Government Plan to Balance the Budget in 2014 While Funding New Initiatives*

Item	Billions of dollars
Total deficit reduction	687
Minus debt service savings	−153
Subtotal	534
Plus funding for new initiatives	41
Total: tax increases and spending cuts to eliminate deficit	575
Changes in the budget	
Revenue change	401
Spending cuts	−175
Defense	−60
Social Security, Medicare, and Medicaid	−47
Other domestic	−68
New spending	41
Foreign affairs	11
Non-defense homeland security	9
Other domestic	21
Net decrease in spending	−134

Sources: Authors' calculations; Congressional Budget Office, "The Budget and Economic Outlook: An Update," August 2003; and chapters 3, 4, 5, and 6.

that it is possible to balance the budget—and produce a better government in the process.

Some observers will conclude that all we have demonstrated is the enormous difficulty of achieving this objective and that the nation might as well learn to live with deficits. The authors of this volume argue that the task is indeed difficult and that, in the end, the nation may not achieve the goal of reducing the deficit to zero. Reducing the deficit to 1 percent of GDP, for example, would be far better than leaving it at 3 percent of GDP. Even so, the authors think it would be a mistake to *plan* to run even modest deficits on a permanent basis. The goal of a balanced budget is well understood by the public, and giving up on this goal would erode fiscal discipline still further.

Improving the Budget Process

We believe that reform of the budget decision process is essential to restoring fiscal discipline. Reducing budget deficits is primarily a matter of political will, but a process that forces politicians to confront hard choices can help. The current process has no teeth and is providing no restraint on spending increases or tax cuts.

Politicians find it easy to vote for more spending and less revenue. Voters who will benefit from these actions are always eager to make their desires known, and the pressure is hard for politicians to withstand. Elected leaders who believe in fiscal discipline and want to avoid deficit spending can benefit from imposing rules on themselves that will force them to consider the deficit consequences of their votes. Conservative politicians have frequently argued that a constitutional amendment requiring Congress to balance the budget would provide political cover that would help politicians resist deficit-increasing actions. It would allow a member of Congress to tell constituents, "I really wanted to vote for your program or your tax cut, but it would have been unconstitutional to do so."

In the mid-1970s Congress implemented budget reforms intended to increase budget discipline by requiring Congress to pass a budget resolution specifying total desired spending, revenues, and deficit or surplus. Debating and passing a budget resolution forced Congress to consider trade-offs among spending programs and tax changes and to decide how large the deficit (or surplus) ought to be. The budget resolution was enforced by various procedures, such as allocations of spending ceilings to appropriations subcommittees, requiring supermajorities to override spending limits, and "reconciliation instructions" that required committees to bring spending and taxing measures into conformity with the budget resolution. Despite these efforts, the reforms did not become successful tools for controlling deficits until they were supplemented by the Budget Enforcement Act (BEA) in 1990. That act established caps in discretionary spending, as well as a set of rules, known as the PAYGO rules, that restrained both mandatory spending and revenue-reducing actions. Essentially, no increase in mandatory spending or tax cut could be brought to the floor for a vote without offsets of an equal amount.

The BEA rules proved extremely effective—helping Congress and the president turn the huge deficits of the early 1990s into substantial surpluses by the end of the decade. The caps made it much harder for Congress to increase discretionary spending. Although caps could be raised—and circumvented by "emergency" spending that did not count against the caps—reluctance to raise them was an effective brake against increases in discretionary spending. The PAYGO rules also restrained increases in mandatory spending and reductions in revenues. The original rules required offsets to any deficit increases over a five-year period—a provision designed to reduce the temptation to enact legislation with modest initial cost (or revenue loss) and larger negative effects on the deficit in the future. When Congress began pushing the deficit impact beyond the five-year window, the period was lengthened to ten years.

Both the Clinton administration and Congress were committed to reducing the deficit, although they differed on how to do it. The discipline of the BEA, combined with the strong economy of the 1990s, helped them make the decisions that eliminated the deficits and produced surpluses for the first time in decades. When the surpluses appeared, however, fiscal discipline soon vanished. Congress began loading up emergency spending bills with items that were in no way emergencies. When the caps and PAYGO rules expired at the end of fiscal year 2002, they were not extended. Congress is now facing huge deficits without an enforcement process to help it make the hard choices.

Budget process reform should involve at least three elements. First, caps on discretionary spending should extend for ten years to discourage pushing costs into the future. In fact, however, caps cannot bind future Congresses if they vote to change them. Second, PAYGO rules should apply both to mandatory spending and to revenue reductions—and should also require ten-year offsets. Moreover, entitlement increases and tax cuts should not be allowed to sunset to make them appear less expensive in the long term. Tax and entitlement changes should normally be considered permanent for purposes of estimating their budget impact. And third, "emergency" spending should be strictly defined. Spending that could have been foreseen should not be allowed to breach the caps or suspend the PAYGO rules. Contingency funds should be budgeted to handle recurrent emergencies, such as forest fires and flooding. Emergency appropriations should require supermajority votes unless accompanied by tax or spending measures that offset their cost.

Variations on these rules are, of course, possible. For example, some favor turning the budget resolution into a law requiring presidential signature. Some would cap total spending, not just discretionary spending. Others would broaden the PAYGO rules so that a tax cut, for example, could be offset by either mandatory or discretionary spending reductions. Many believe that an item veto, if it could be designed to be constitutional, would help the president enforce budget discipline. The main point, however, is that spending and tax cutting are out of control and the budget process needs to be reinvigorated to help stiffen the resolve of politicians to act in a fiscally responsible manner.

Moreover, as detailed in chapter 5, deficit pressures will mount rapidly as the baby boom generation claims its retirement benefits and longevity continues to increase. These future liabilities, which can be quite accurately estimated in advance, should be reflected in the budget to underline the importance of taking immediate steps to bring future budgets into balance.

Notes

1. Stephen Slivinski, "The Corporate Welfare Budget: Bigger Than Ever," Cato Institute Policy Analysis 415 (Washington, October 10, 2001). We derive the savings for 2014 specified in table 2-3 by adjusting the savings of the Cato cuts by inflation and population growth.

2. Committee on the Budget, U.S. House of Representatives, "Government Waste, Fraud, and Abuse Update" (October 2003).

3. Congressional Budget Office, *Budget Options* (March 2003).

4. This conclusion is arrived at as follows. Reducing the deficit in 2014 would require $534 billion in new revenues or spending cuts. Most of the candidates proposed health care plans that would cost roughly $100 billion a year or more by that date. Their proposals to provide greater funding for education ("full funding for special education, more access to preschool and higher education") would likely cost another $60 billion at a minimum. Added to the funds needed for deficit reduction and for other proposed initiatives, the total cost would be in the neighborhood of $700 billion a year.

5. The costs of these proposals over a ten-year period are estimated to vary from $6.1 trillion for Dennis Kucinich's plan to a little under $1 trillion for the Kerry plan. Kucinich created a single-payer plan that would extend Medicare benefits to the entire population and pay for it with a 7.7 percent payroll tax on employers. Kerry would rely more heavily on augmenting existing public programs, such as Medicaid and the Children's Health Insurance Plan (CHIP), and would provide individual tax credits to offset premium costs among the middle class. See Sara R. Collins, Karen Davis, and Jeanne M. Lambrew, "Health Care

Reform Returns to the National Agenda: The 2004 Presidential Candidates' Proposals" (New York: Commonwealth Fund, September 2003, updated February 20, 2004).

6. John Edwards's proposal to bolster the Pell grant system of financial assistance to college students would cost about $3 billion annually (available at www.johnedwards2004.com/education.asp). Providing high-quality preschool to all low-income children would cost about $30 billion a year. Isabel Sawhill, "Investing in Children," Brookings Children's Roundtable Policy Brief 1 (April 1999), p. 7.

7. National Education Association, "IDEA Funding Coalition Offers Proposal" (www.nea.org/specialed/coalitionfunding2002.html). NEA data through 2010; for 2011–14, annual spending growth of 3.5 percent is assumed.

3

Reassessing National Security

LAEL BRAINARD AND
MICHAEL O'HANLON

Two years after September 11, 2001—with two major military operations undertaken, two uncertain nation-building ventures under
way, and the risk of a deadly combination of terrorism, rogue regimes, and
weapons of mass destruction still unacceptably high—security remains at
the top of the nation's agenda. The war on terrorism has not only greatly
expanded spending on security, but also introduced great uncertainty into
the ten-year budget outlook—uncertainty that argues for humility in estimating future spending. The budget for national security has grown by
roughly $200 billion above anticipated needs in just two and a half years
and has been the primary contributor to the expansion of federal spending during that time. In fiscal 2004 alone, supplemental requests outside
the normal budget cycle expanded the national security budget by almost
one-fifth.[1] Nonetheless, one thing is clear: at this moment in history, we
cannot afford to shortchange America's security.

The authors are grateful to Gordon Adams, Susan Rice, and Jim Steinberg for
extremely thoughtful comments and to Una Lee for excellent research assistance.

America's security has three critical, interdependent components: military force, homeland security, and the softer tools of diplomacy and foreign assistance. This chapter thus addresses military power, homeland security, and foreign affairs as integral parts of a *unified national security budget*, even as it delves into detail on each separately so as to respect U.S. federal accounting conventions and recognize the distinctive qualities of each of these major activities. The unified analysis confirms that the three critical components of national security policy are mostly complements rather than substitutes. But the analysis also highlights the potential for a stronger civilian capacity to share some of the burden undertaken by the U.S. military in the increasingly important area of complex emergencies and postconflict reconstruction.

The United States today confronts new threats that could prove as sustained as the totalitarian challenges of the previous half-century. A smart strategy to address the challenges to national security from radical extremism, killer diseases, uneven globalization, and states that fail their own people would further expand real resources for homeland security, foreign aid, and diplomacy. It could be combined with a deceleration of growth in defense spending, but only under optimistic assumptions of greater foreign burden sharing, an eventual withdrawal of forces from Iraq and Afghanistan combined with no new massive engagements abroad, and an efficient allocation of military resources. Such a scenario could see total spending on national security growing, on average, by roughly 1.2 percent a year in real terms but still remaining $40 billion below the adjusted baseline projection of $737.4 billion in 2014 (table 3-1).[2]

The U.S. Armed Forces

What military will the United States need in 2014, and how much will it cost? Answering these questions is difficult because the United States simply does not know what type of world it will find in a decade. Assuming that today's international environment will persist in 2014 would be foolish. No one can easily forecast either the state of the struggle against global terror at that date or the state of U.S. international relations. Thus this analysis must be speculative. Rather than develop different scenarios

Table 3-1. *Projected and Recommended Spending on National Security*
Billions of dollars

	Spending in 2003	Projected spending in 2014	Recommended spending in 2014	Change in spending in 2014
Defense	407.0	649.0	589.0	–60.0
Homeland security, total spending	32.0	56.0	65.0	9.0
Defense[a]	11.0	16.0	16.0	0.0
Non-defense	22.0	40.0	49.0	9.0
Foreign affairs[b]	33.0	48.4	59.6	11.2
Total	462.0	737.4	697.6	–39.8

Source: Authors' calculations; Congressional Budget Office, "The Budget and Economic Outlook: An Update," August 2003; and Office of Management and Budget, *Historical Tables, Budget of the US Government, Fiscal Year 2004* (2003), p. 83.
a. Part of homeland security spending is included in the defense budget, as shown.
b. Foreign affairs and non-defense homeland security are customarily included in non-defense discretionary spending.

for several radically different geostrategic environments, it postulates circumstances that seem most likely. Six assumptions guide the analysis. First, in 2014, America's existing alliances, which account for more than 80 percent of world military spending, will still be intact and functioning well, despite the strains of recent years (most notably during the Bush presidency). Second, relations with China, Russia, and India will generally be peaceful (the Bush record here is rather good), but conflict could erupt in all three neighborhoods, and the United States could be drawn in too (especially in the Taiwan Strait). Third, by 2014, the Iraq occupation will be over, and that country will be at relative peace. But extremism, state-sponsored terrorism, and political instability will continue to imperil the broader region. Fourth, North Korea will remain a threat, even if increasingly weak by conventional measures vis-à-vis South Korea. Fifth, major conflict could still erupt between India and Pakistan. Sixth, failed states will still pose not just a major humanitarian concern but a worry in the ongoing struggle against terror, necessitating serious attention to peacekeeping and nation building.

The main premise of this chapter, however, is that, for all its flaws, the U.S.-led alliance system and a strong American military are essential. Absent a strong American security role, regions such as the Persian Gulf and Northeast Asia could easily endure more severe conflict, global oil flows could be disrupted, more states could develop nuclear weapons out of fear for their own security, and more wars could flare among states.

Given these assumptions and objectives, can the United States maintain good national security at reasonable cost? We believe that an average annual real growth of 0.8 percent in defense spending, resulting in $589 billion in spending in 2014, could yield a defense budget adequate to meet U.S. responsibilities (table 3-1)—but only if the United States makes smart and economical choices about weapons modernization and finally figures out how to save money in defense support activities, and if allies pick up a larger share of the collective cost of projecting force to trouble spots overseas. Otherwise, the real defense budget could easily exceed $650 billion if not $700 billion in 2014.

Background

Whether U.S. defense spending is judged high or low depends on how it is measured. Compared with spending in other countries, it is enormous, nearly half of aggregate global military spending. Compared with the nation's cold war norms, it is on the higher side of spending over the past half century, though not out of bounds. Relative to the size of the American economy, by contrast, defense spending alone remains quite modest at under 4 percent of GDP (less than half to two-thirds of typical cold war levels).

Certainly in terms of personnel, the current U.S. defense establishment is not large. U.S. troop levels and most types of military force structure are one-third smaller than they were in the later cold war years, just over half the size of China's military, and not that much larger than those of India, Russia, and North Korea. Nevertheless, that force is extensively engaged around the world—with roughly 100,000 troops in Europe, again as many in Asia, and more than 150,000 in the Persian Gulf region.

Republicans and Democrats generally agree about the broad contours of American force levels and weaponry. Secretary Donald Rumsfeld's 2001 Quadrennial Defense Review reaffirmed the active-duty troop levels of about 1.4 million maintained during the Clinton administration and also retained most of the Clinton agenda for weapons modernization. After September 11, Rumsfeld sought and received a great deal more budget authority than President Clinton's defense plan called for, but a Democratic president would almost certainly also have boosted defense spending to cover shortfalls in funding the previous plan. That Rumsfeld retained most Clinton era ideas and programs is relatively unsurprising. Although decisions to buy specific weapons can be debated, the military needs many new or refurbished planes, ships, and ground vehicles because much of the weaponry bought during the Reagan buildup is wearing out. America's technological edge in combat may not require every weapon now in development or production, but the advantages to maintaining a resounding superiority in weaponry are evidenced in the rapid victories and relatively low casualties (on all sides) in Bosnia, Kosovo, Afghanistan, and Iraq. And talk of cutting back on ground forces during the early Rumsfeld tenure has stopped—at least for the foreseeable future—given the challenges posed by postwar Iraq.

Even once the Iraq mission winds down, as it most likely will well before 2014, there will not be unlimited room for programmatic and budgetary maneuver. Since the cold war ended, U.S. armed forces have been designed to be able to fight two full-scale wars at once. Rumsfeld modified the requirement in 2001 so that only one of the victories needed to be immediate and overwhelming. But the basic logic of the idea was retained—and should be retained even assuming the successful stabilization of post-Saddam Iraq. A two-war capability of some sort permits the United States to fight one war without letting down its guard everywhere else, which would undercut deterrence and perhaps increase the likelihood of a secondary conflict. In addition, smaller but longer force deployments for missions such as postwar stabilization cannot be excluded and could even number two or three at a time, as they do now.

What forces does the United States need for such possible wars? At least one possible conflict—war in Korea—could closely resemble the U.S. deployment (including half a million troops) for Operation Desert Storm in 1991. Another, war against China in the Taiwan Strait, would likely require roughly the air and naval capability deployed to Operation Desert Storm but far less ground power, and total personnel requirements in the range of 150,000 to 200,000.[3] Stability scenarios and peacekeeping missions in South Asia or Southeast Asia or Africa could plausibly require 100,000 or more Americans. Despite sophisticated innovations in warfighting, as we have been reminded of late in Iraq, such missions are often dominated by fairly mundane and timeless requirements for "boots on the ground."

In a world in which American national security interests make it urgent to prevent states from failing—and providing refuge and resources to groups like al Qaeda—it may not be possible to debate reducing U.S. ground forces anytime soon. Indeed, a strong case can be made that in the short term the United States needs more ground forces, not fewer, and that it will have to shift more of the burden for ground force operations to its active-duty forces rather than its reserve component (today, Army reserve elements contain slightly more personnel than active-duty forces).

Constraining Future Defense Budgets

The basic logic of the high-quality military personnel, technological pre-eminence, two-war capability, global deterrent posture, and engagement strategy that drives the size of the American armed forces and hence their budget is sound. But are there practical ways to cap defense spending? If not, not only the country's domestic agenda but even its long-term security could be damaged, as the underpinnings of national prosperity and power are eroded.

In particular, there may be realistic means to limit the real growth of the U.S. defense budget to less than what we view here as the adjusted baseline—that is, current spending levels adjusted for inflation and population growth. In other words, inflation-adjusted defense spending would still increase, but not as fast as the economy and not nearly as fast as in recent years. Achieving this goal will take some innovative policy ideas, some good fortune, and cooperation from friends and allies. But it may be achievable, and the rough contours of how that would be done are sketched out below.

First, though, to get a rough sense of what is feasible within the Pentagon budget, it is worth noting that while several factors push defense spending up faster than that 0.8 percent real growth level, several may also permit slower (or even zero) growth. Keeping these factors in mind makes it easier to see why 0.8 percent annual real growth is probably the right general frame of reference within which to project future defense spending.

Historically, real operating costs per uniformed individual have grown by 2 percent to 3 percent a year. Weapons costs have grown comparably. Rising health care and environmental cleanup costs affect the military as much as any other sector of the economy. And to attract top-notch people, military pay increases must keep up with civilian pay, which can require average real growth of at least 0.8 percent a year.

Several other realities offer some hope of savings. Greater use of relatively inexpensive high-technology computers and electronics can allow rapid improvements in military capabilities at modest cost. Defense efficiencies through privatization and other reforms may save at least modest sums. And greater assistance from allies may reduce overall demands on American forces, especially over a ten-year period like that being considered here.

It should also be noted that the direct military costs of the war on terror, while large, are not astronomical. Leaving aside the one-time mission in Iraq, they include about $10 billion a year in added costs for military base security, less than $5 billion in Defense Department contributions to homeland security, less than $10 billion a year in offensive counterterrorist missions, and about $5 billion in added intelligence costs. That total of less than $30 billion a year is substantial but less than half the overall increase in real defense spending since 9/11 (not even counting the costs of the Iraq mission today). Moreover, absent another major interstate war related to terrorism, some of the above numbers may decrease with time.

More Burden Sharing?

Today the United States outspends its major allies by about 2 to 1 but outdistances them in military force that can be projected overseas and sustained there by a ratio of at least 5 to 1. Most American allies spent the cold war preparing to defend their own or nearby territories against a Soviet threat, while American forces focused on how to deploy and operate forces many thousands of miles from home. Most U.S. allies have gotten serious about this effort only since the cold war ended (if at all).

Shifting defense responsibilities to our allies is an attractive idea—but it is not really our choice. And near-term prospects for success are not good. Although many U.S. allies have good militaries, strong military traditions, and a high-tech industrial base, political obstacles to defense buildups are formidable. Several European countries face large fiscal deficits. Other nations believe, perhaps wishfully, that force is less important today than it once was. Incentives to free-ride on U.S. capabilities are strong. European nations also often cite, with some justification, their large peacekeeping forces. Germany and Japan are disinclined to remilitarize, and their former adversaries, including many Americans, hesitate to dissuade them.

Some progress has been made. European militaries are developing the combined capacity to deploy up to 60,000 troops afar and to sustain them there for a year. Japan is slowly enlarging its interpretation of which military missions are consistent with its post–World War II constitution. U.S., British, and French programs are slowly helping African militaries improve their skills. And the recent transatlantic quarrel over Iraq may spur European countries to strengthen their militaries to gain more clout in global decisionmaking about the use of force. Reallocating about 10 percent of current major allied military spending could give other industrialized countries fully half as much deployable military capability as the United States within a decade—if they have the political will.[4] If they could summon that will, U.S. forces might shrink modestly with completion of the Iraq mission, assuming the world were to stay at least moderately stable. Reductions in military manpower of a few percent would be needed to hold spending to the planned 0.8 percent annual real growth yearly level.

Emphasizing Advanced Electronics and Computers in Defense Modernization

One reason the Pentagon budget is slated to grow so much in coming years—with real increases closer to 2 percent a year than the 0.8 percent targeted here—has to do with buying weaponry. Some of the upward pressure arises from high-profile issues such as missile defense. But most comes from the main combat systems, which are generally wearing out. Living off the fruits of the Reagan military buildup, the Clinton administration—generally a rather good custodian of the American armed forces—spent an average of $50 billion a year on equipment, only about 15 percent of the defense budget, as against a historical norm of about 25 percent. This "procurement holiday" is about over. The procurement budget climbed to $70 billion in 2003 and is slated to reach $100 billion in 2009 (in constant 2003 dollars)—thus regaining its historical norm in real terms.

Some of this budget increase is needed, given aging weapons and the imperative of adding new capabilities such as at least a modest ballistic and cruise missile defense capability. But the Pentagon's plan may be excessive. Despite Bush's presidential election campaign promise to "skip a generation" of weaponry, his Pentagon has canceled only one major weapon system—the Army's Crusader howitzer, which was not even particularly expensive. Although procurement budgets must continue rising, economies can almost certainly be found through expanded applications of modestly priced technologies, such as the smart weapons and communications systems that starred in Afghanistan. Such cost-cutting measures, too, will be needed to hold real Defense Department budget growth to 0.8 percent a year on average.

The Bush plan lacks clear priorities. Like the Clinton administration, it proposes to replace major combat systems *throughout* the force structure with systems costing twice as much. A more discriminating and economy-minded modernization strategy would equip only a portion of the armed forces with the most sophisticated and expensive major weapons platforms, including ships, planes, and ground vehicles. That high-end component would hedge against new exigencies, such as an unexpectedly rapid modernization of the Chinese military. The rest of the military establishment would be equipped primarily with relatively inexpensive upgrades of existing weaponry, including better sensors, munitions, computers, and communications systems. Such an approach would not keep the procurement budget in the $70–75 billion range. But it might hold it to $80–85 billion a year instead of $100 billion or more.

Operations and Maintenance

All defense planners would love to save money in the relatively unglamorous but critical parts of the Pentagon budget known as operations and maintenance. These accounts, which pay for a wide range of activities, including training, overseas deployments, upkeep of equipment, military base operations, and health care costs—in short, for near-term military readiness—have been rising fast in recent years, and it will be hard to stop the overall upward trend.[5]

Some specific savings are already in the works. Congress has agreed to authorize another round of base closures in 2005.[6] Since the cold war's end, U.S. military forces have shrunk by more than one-third, yet domestic base capacity has fallen only 20 percent. Once completed, retrenchment of base capacity will save at least $4 billion annually. Overhauling military health care services by merging the independent health plans of each military service and introducing a small copayment for military personnel and their families could save $2 billion or more a year, though these steps would be controversial.[7] Other savings in operations and maintenance are possible. For example, encouraging local base commanders to economize by letting them keep some of the savings they might generate for their base activities could save a billion dollars a year or more within a decade.[8]

All that said, these accounts are crucial to national security and have proved tough to cap or contain. Privatization is no panacea; it takes time and generally saves much less than its warmest advocates assert. But if overall operating costs can be held to a 0.8 percent real rise instead of the historical norm exceeding 2 percent, the budget path envisioned here may be within reach.

Homeland Security

Since the attacks of September 11, 2001, much has been done to improve the safety of Americans, not only in the offensive war on terror abroad but in protecting the homeland as well. Americans, aware now of the harm terrorists can inflict, are on alert, providing a first, crucial line of defense. Air travel is much safer. Intelligence sharing, especially regarding individuals suspected of ties to terrorism, has improved. Suspicious ships entering U.S. waters are screened more frequently. Steps have been taken to reduce the country's exposure to biological attacks, and oversight has

been tightened on labs working with biological materials. Private terrorism insurance is now backstopped by a new federal program. Well-known
bridges, tunnels, and nuclear reactors are protected by police and
National Guard forces when terrorism alerts so advise.

But much remains to be done. Most of the above steps respond to past
tactics of al Qaeda rather than anticipating new ways that al Qaeda or
other terrorist groups might try to harm Americans. Part of the answer is
to continue to build the new Department of Homeland Security (DHS),
especially those elements involved with border security, intelligence, and
the federal government's interactions with state, local, and private efforts
to improve the country's safety.

Far more urgent than creating a new bureaucracy, however, is filling
the gaps that remain in the current homeland security effort. These range
from creating a new networked intelligence capability to anticipate and
prevent future terrorist actions, to better protecting private infrastructure
like chemical plants and skyscrapers, to strengthening the Coast Guard
and Customs (within DHS). They also include making sure first respon-
ders can communicate over commonly accessible radio networks during
emergencies, hastening development of port security plans, and improving security of transportation networks aside from airports.[9]

It is not possible to stop every type of terrorist violence. But by focusing on preventing catastrophic attacks, the United States can approach
homeland security systematically and with a better chance of preventing
future attacks on the scale of the 9/11 tragedy. That will take more attention from Congress and the administration—and more money, perhaps
$10 billion a year (less than 3 percent of the defense budget) above what
the administration proposed to spend a year ago, for a total of about
$65 billion in 2014 in federal funding.

Homeland security is daunting in its complexity and in the sheer number of potential terrorist targets in an open country of nearly 300 million
people. As such, it requires a conceptual foundation and set of priorities.
Recognizing as much, the Bush administration put forth a strategy for
homeland security on July 16, 2002.[10] Acknowledging that terrorists are
themselves strategic, adaptive actors who will pursue new modes of
attack and new weaponry, including weapons of mass destruction, the
strategy emphasizes the crucial roles played by state and local govern-

ments as well as the private sector and individual citizens. Indeed, according to administration estimates, of about $100 billion a year in total national spending on homeland security today, the federal share is only about $40 billion.

The Bush administration approach involves six "critical mission areas": intelligence and warning, border and transportation security, domestic counterterrorism, protecting critical infrastructures and key assets, defending against catastrophic threats, and emergency preparedness and response. The administration also proposed four key methods, or "foundations," for enhancing all six areas: law, science and technology, information sharing and systems, and international cooperation. The administration's strategy makes a start, but it leaves out four key priorities for action. One is major infrastructure in the private sector, which the Bush administration largely ignores. A second is information technology and its proper uses, especially information sharing in government at all levels and between the public and private sectors. A third is the unrecognized need to expand greatly certain specific capacities for homeland security, such as the Coast Guard and Customs, as well as security for forms of transportation, such as trains. The fourth is intelligence reforms, especially the ability to monitor terrorists and to anticipate where their next attacks may come. Here the administration has fallen short. Incredibly, it has to date not even fully integrated the various suspected terrorist watch lists of various agencies.

Expanding these capacities in existing federal agencies will require more money, though far less than for the post–September 11 defense buildup. But annual funding for this federal responsibility, which has already doubled from roughly $20 billion to $40 billion, needs to grow further, to about $65 billion in 2014, if the country is to take reasonable precautions against future terrorist attacks that could be at least as destructive as those of 2001.

"Soft Power:" The Foreign Affairs Budget

Even before September 11, 2001, many thoughtful observers worried that the United States was underinvesting in the nonmilitary tools of foreign policy.[11] Although funding has since increased substantially, we believe that there is still a compelling case for expansion relative to the CBO baseline projection to effectively address infectious diseases such as HIV/AIDS and malaria, global poverty, complex emergencies, and America's new strategic interests. In many cases, such as the HIV/AIDS pandemic and the reconstruction of war-torn states, greater commitments of resources early on can diminish the overall cost to the U.S. taxpayer. And U.S. resources can also be leveraged by making the extra effort to build international support.

Foreign Affairs Spending in Historical Context

Over the past four decades, U.S. foreign assistance has been driven primarily by traditional national security priorities, especially the cold war and developments in the Middle East. The end of the cold war, disillusionment with aid's many failures, and the drive to balance the budget produced a slash-and-burn approach to the foreign affairs budget during the 1990s. Today American spending on foreign aid, never generous, looks paltry compared with that of many other wealthy nations. Although the United States is one of the top two donors in absolute terms (Japan is the other), it spends less relative to its income than any other wealthy nation. At 0.1 percent of GDP, U.S. official development assistance is less than half the industrial country average of 0.22 percent.[12] Per capita, U.S. aid of $35 a year is far below the industrial country average of $62.[13]

Several recent developments argue strongly for increased spending on foreign aid. First, American resources are absolutely critical to combat the HIV/AIDS pandemic, a humanitarian tragedy of epic proportions that threatens to reverse impressive gains on child survival and health, life expectancy, productivity, and literacy in the world's poorest countries. Second, the acceleration of globalization has raised growing concern that unless the benefits are better shared, the divide between rich and poor could contribute to civil conflict, extremism, conflict over resources, and environmental degradation. Third, activists have developed a powerful recipe for mobilizing public support for greater international giving by focusing on a simple and compelling goal and enlisting high-profile public champions to help forge coalitions across the political spectrum. Finally, the post–September 11 war on terrorism has greatly expanded the strategic calls on foreign aid—directly to reward allies, shore up frontline states, and rebuild Afghanistan and Iraq and indirectly to address the poverty that weakens states and provides space for terrorist networks to grow.

Although foreign aid is a central component of U.S. national security policy, spending on aid has lagged far behind the "hard" dimensions of security since September 11, 2001. For example, for fiscal year 2004, the administration requested an increase of $96 billion, or 31 percent, for defense;[14] an increase of $24.4 billion, or 185 percent, for homeland security;[15] and an increase of just $5 billion, or 22 percent, for foreign affairs, relative to fiscal 2000.[16]

Major Programs in the Foreign Affairs Budget

Conceptually, foreign affairs spending can be divided into seven main programmatic categories. Table 3-2 shows spending on the main components of the foreign affairs account in fiscal 2003, what spending would be in 2014 if the account were to grow in line with inflation and U.S. population growth (the adjusted baseline scenario) if the programmatic shares remained the same, and our recommended spending for 2014. We believe that the new imperatives associated with combating killer diseases, global terrorism, and global poverty warrant higher growth in the foreign affairs account than elsewhere in the budget. But given how little the United States spends on foreign affairs and given projected declines in selected major components, our recommended increase is only about $11 billion above the baseline in 2014.

Although 40 percent of the foreign affairs budget—the development, trade, and investment and the politically allocated assistance categories—support economic activities, most of this is allocated among countries based on political considerations.[17] Only about 10 percent of the foreign affairs budget is spent on development assistance in the strict sense that it is allocated according to primarily economic criteria.[18] Development aid has recently received a boost from two directions. First, the growing consensus surrounding the urgency of the HIV/AIDS pandemic and our abil-

Table 3-2. *Major Program Areas in the Foreign Affairs Budget*
Billions of dollars, unless otherwise noted

Type of assistance	Spending in 2003	Share of foreign affairs spending in 2003 (percent)	Projected spending in 2014	Recommended spending in 2014
Total	33.0	100.0	48.4	59.6
Development, trade, and investment	6.6	20.2	9.8	27.5
Politically allocated assistance	6.6	20.3	9.8	8.4
Humanitarian assistance	1.6	4.8	2.3	2.3
Security assistance	6.8	20.7	10.0	10.5
International organizations and programs	1.1	3.2	1.6	1.4
Complex emergencies[a]	4.3	13.0	6.3	1.7
Diplomacy	5.9	17.9	8.6	7.8

Source: Authors' calculations; Public Law 108-7; "Making Further Continuing Appropriations for the Fiscal Year 2003"; and Public Law 108-11, "Emergency Wartime Supplemental Appropriations Act, 2003."

a. The category complex emergencies includes funds allocated to Iraq Relief and Reconstruction, the Office of Transition Initiatives, the President's Fund for Complex Emergencies, Emergency Refugee and Migration Assistance, and funds related to reconstruction/relief activities in Afghanistan and Kosovo.

ity to effectively contain and combat it have expanded spending in this area. Second, the administration has proposed a large, permanent increase in bilateral development assistance of $5 billion a year by fiscal 2006, allocated through a new, more flexible and performance-oriented program, the Millennium Challenge Account (MCA).[19]

Projecting to 2014, there are a variety of external estimates of the total price tag for combating global poverty and HIV/AIDS. The midrange of estimates of the cost of achieving the internationally agreed UN Millennium Development Goals for poverty reduction and human development (including fighting HIV/AIDS) implies a global increase of $65.6 billion over current expenditures by 2014.[20] We recommend that the United States assume a share of this burden in proportion to its share of OECD income,[21] which would imply a total U.S. contribution of $23.8 billion in 2014 (on top of existing programs in investment and trade), sufficient to fully fund the MCA and significantly increase funding for HIV/AIDS and growth and poverty reduction more broadly. While this increase would require significantly more resources in 2014 than the adjusted baseline assumptions, it is a sound investment that should yield dividends not only from a humanitarian perspective but also in boosting America's perceived legitimacy abroad and thus helping to advance our agenda internationally. In many other categories of the foreign affairs budget, there is reason to expect spending to grow in line with or below the adjusted baseline projection. Both politically allocated economic assistance and security assistance for foreign military training and capabilities, which together account for more than 40 percent of foreign affairs spending, are slated to decline under agreements negotiated with Egypt and Israel, the largest recipients.[22] Assistance to former Warsaw Pact countries can also be expected to decline.[23] For humanitarian assistance, where public support is generally strong, the baseline scenario is compatible with growth in line with inflation and world population growth.[24]

Since September 11, 2001, with growing concern that the United States is losing the battle of hearts and minds in the Islamic world, numerous task forces have called for substantial expansion of U.S. public diplomacy. Spending on diplomacy, which we define to include all State Department operational costs and public information activities, including broadcasting, has recently received a significant boost to upgrade embassy security, following declines in the 1990s. Although we support the calls for improved public diplomacy, even big expansions to these programs would have little impact on the overall budget, because of their relatively modest cost.

Overall, the foreign affairs account of the U.S. budget measures the priority America places on the exercise of diplomacy and foreign assistance. Over the next ten years, there is good reason to expect and indeed support continued real expansion in foreign affairs spending to combat threats to our national security from the HIV/AIDS crisis, global poverty, and global terrorism.

Strengthening the Civilian Response to Complex Emergencies

One other area of the foreign affairs budget—complex emergencies, and particularly postconflict reconstruction—requires more comment. Although candidate Bush derided U.S. forays into "nation building" during the 2000 election, just four years later the United States is engaged in two new and ambitious (particularly in the case of Iraq) such exercises.

This follows on four postconflict reconstruction projects initiated in the past decade alone (one under the first President Bush, making the endeavor fully bipartisan).[25] Like it or not, stabilization and transition in postconflict societies are likely to remain unavoidable U.S. responsibilities. Failing to prepare for this reality would be negligent and shortsighted.

We recommend strengthening budget resources and programmatic coherence for complex emergencies, an area where the potential for overlap between military and civilian capabilities is high.[26] In Iraq as elsewhere, the United States often asks the military to do things that are largely civilian in nature, simply because it is better equipped to respond quickly and to find the necessary resources to fund unanticipated missions. This is efficient for some "dual-use" capabilities, where replicating capacity in a civilian agency separate from the Department of Defense would be hugely redundant and costly (the scale can run to tens of thousands of soldiers). But in situations where the U.S. military is not deployed and in stabilized postconflict environments, it would be more cost effective to draw on a stand-by capacity of perhaps 500 to 1,000 civilians capable of quickly undertaking efforts to aid and rebuild countries in distress. In Iraq, for example, it makes little sense for the Pentagon to execute multibillion-dollar development and reconstruction contracts for the country's electricity grid, phone network, or highway system. Similarly, in the southern sectors of Iraq, where the U.S. armed forces are not present, multinational divisions in place do not have adequate spare logistical capacity to handle even the immediate postwar economic and humanitarian activities.

We therefore advocate creating, within the State Department's Agency for International Development, an integrated office to respond quickly to complex humanitarian emergencies, which might merge and expand the existing capabilities of the Offices of Foreign Disaster Assistance and Transition Initiatives and related units with the effect of creating new standing capacity ready to react quickly. The individuals in this office would not be so numerous as to rebuild a country on their own; rather, they would develop and oversee the execution of plans to rebuild a country or address other complex emergencies, relying on private contractors from the United States and abroad as well as nongovernmental organizations.

Congress routinely and understandably rejects administration requests for standing funds for contingencies as "slush funds," instead financing these operations through often slow and cumbersome supplemental budget requests. Congress could prepare for more rapid and cost-effective interventions by underwriting a stand-by civilian capacity with modest contingency funding, which could be scaled up rapidly through emergency supplemental funding. Congress has taken a step in this direction with its recent decision to grant the administration's request for a $100 million contingency fund.

The cost of such a new program would be modest, perhaps a few hundred million dollars with an additional $100 million annually if the United States also created a dedicated police force of up to 1,000 officers for deployment to postconflict zones—a critical need in recent crises.

Using adjusted baseline assumptions, we project spending on all programs currently addressing complex emergencies to be $6.3 billion in 2014.[27] Although America's reconstruction spending in Afghanistan and Iraq should taper off by 2014, sharply reducing spending in this category, the importance of preventing failed states in an age of global terror adds a hard-headed security rationale to an already compelling humanitarian case for devoting adequate resources to complex emergencies. Thus, for 2014, we suggest that non–Defense Department U.S. spending on complex emergencies could be twice the average of U.S. spending between 1999 and 2003 (when civilian costs were low and military costs were dominant), amounting to $1.7 billion, including the costs of a standing civilian agency. A more deliberate approach to dividing up responsibilities between military and civilian personnel might also entail some reallocation between the defense and foreign affairs accounts.[28]

Conclusion

Even in these difficult fiscal times, the United States needs to spend more on its foreign policy and national security activities broadly defined. The state of the world and the country's national security interests require it. Indeed, in real-dollar terms, the United States should make further modest increases in all three major budgetary elements of its national security activities—the armed forces, homeland security, and international affairs—which means that in real-dollar terms future spending levels will attain the peak levels of the cold war.

The nation surely can afford this, however, given the growth of its economy since the cold war. In that sense, the 1990s post–cold war peace dividend will not be entirely lost. Defense budgets, which ranged from 5 percent to 10 percent of GDP during the cold war, could remain comfortably below 4 percent and need only grow slightly faster than inflation to address likely demands of the strategic environment. The federal homeland security budget, less than $20 billion annually before 9/11 and now about $30 billion, needs to increase further to roughly $65 billion. But even that will represent less than half a percent of GDP. International affairs budgets for diplomacy and aid, while needing much larger relative increases (given their scant funding in recent years), would rise to $60 billion in total. Nonetheless there is a compelling argument for an even greater investment in foreign affairs and diplomacy to advance the nation's strategic interests and to address moral and humanitarian imperatives. Foreign affairs spending has fallen as a share of the budget from 5.3 percent of total outlays in 1962 at the time of the Cuban missile crisis to just 1.3 percent in 2000, and as a share of national income from 1 percent in 1962 to 0.2 percent in 2000.[29] Even the recommended annual growth rate of roughly 3 percent would still keep foreign affairs shares at less than one-third of what they were during the cold war. In sum, the total cost of all three main pillars of American foreign policy will be less than 4 percent of GDP and less than 20 percent of total federal spending.

In today's fiscal climate, asking for any increases in federal funding at all is admittedly a difficult proposition. But the U.S. struggle against terrorism, killer diseases, global poverty, and other dangerous problems demands it. The challenges posed by exploding populations in most of the world's poorest regions, major schisms between the Islamic and non-Islamic worlds, and globalization demand that we treat this issue with the utmost urgency—even as the memories of September 11 and associated political pressure to improve the defenses of the country may begin to lose some of the strength they possessed just three short years ago.

Notes

1. Authors' calculations based on Office of Management and Budget, *Historical Tables, Budget of the U.S. Government, Fiscal Year 2004* (2003), and Office of Management and Budget, "FY04 Supplemental: Iraq and Afghanistan Ongoing Operations/Reconstruction" (2003) (available at www.whitehouse.gov/omb/budget/amendments/supplemental_9_17_03.pdf).

2. The 1.2 percent real growth rate was constructed using average annual inflation of 2.6 percent over 2003–14.

3. Michael O'Hanlon, *Defense Policy Choices for the Bush Administration*, rev. ed. (Brookings, 2002).

4. For backup on those estimates, see John E. Peters and Howard Deshong, *Out of Area or Out of Reach? European Military Support for Operations in Southwest Asia* (Santa Monica, Calif.: RAND, 1995); Michael O'Hanlon, "Transforming NATO: The Role of European Forces," *Survival*, vol. 39, no. 3 (Autumn 1997), pp. 5–15; Congressional Budget Office, *NATO Burdensharing after Enlargement* (2001).

5. Gregory T. Kiley, "The Effects of Aging on the Costs of Operating and Maintaining Military Equipment" (Congressional Budget Office, August 2001); Congressional Budget Office, *Paying for Military Readiness and Upkeep: Trends in Operation and Maintenance Spending* (1997).

6. Some optimists tend to exaggerate the savings from possible base closings, however. Congressional Budget Office, *Closing Military Bases: An Interim Assessment* (1996).

7. See Congressional Budget Office, *Restructuring Military Medical Care* (1995); Congressional Budget Office, *Accrual Budgeting for Military Retirees' Health Care* (2002).

8. Robert F. Hale, *Promoting Efficiency in the Department of Defense: Keep Trying, but Be Realistic* (Washington: Center for Strategic and Budgetary Assessments, 2002).

9. See Jack Weiss, *Preparing Los Angeles for Terrorism* (City of Los Angeles, October 2002).

10. See Office of Homeland Security, *National Strategy for Homeland Security* (July 2002), available at www.whitehouse.gov.

11. We borrow the term "soft power" from Joseph Nye. "Soft power lies in the ability to attract and persuade rather than coerce. It means that others want what the United States wants, and there is less need to use carrots and sticks. Hard power, the ability to coerce, grows out of a country's military and economic might. Soft power arises from the attractiveness of a country's culture, political ideals, and policies." Joseph S. Nye Jr., "U.S. Power and Strategy after Iraq," *Foreign Affairs*, vol. 82, no. 4 (July/August 2003), p. 66. Here we use the term broadly to encompass foreign assistance and diplomacy.

12. Lael Brainard, Carol Graham, Nigel Purvis, Steven Radelet, and Gayle Smith, *The Other War: Global Poverty and the Millennium Challenge Account* (Brookings, 2003), p. 197.

13. Ibid.

14. Authors' calculations based on Office of Management and Budget, *Historical Tables*, p. 83.

15. Office of Management and Budget, "FY 2004 Budget Fact Sheet" (2003), available at www.whitehouse.gov/news/releases/2003/10/20031001-7.html, and Office of Management and Budget, *Securing the Homeland and Strengthening the Nation* (2002), p. 8.

16. Authors' calculations based on Bureau of Resource Management, *Summary and Highlights: International Affairs (Function 150) Fiscal Year 2004 Budget Request* (U.S. Department of State, 2003), available at http://state.gov/m/rm/rls/iab.

17. Authors' calculations and Public Law 108-7, "Making Further Continuing Appropriations for the Fiscal Year 2003," and PL 108-11, "Emergency Wartime Supplemental Appropriations Act, 2003."

18. Ibid.

19. Brainard and others, *The Other War*, p. 3.

20. Authors' calculations based on United Nations Development Program, *Human Development Report 2003* (Oxford University Press, 2003), p.146.

21. Organization for Economic Cooperation and Development, *OECD Economic Outlook No. 73 Statistical Annex Tables* (2003).

22. Authors' calculations based on Bureau of Resource Management, *Summary and Highlights*; and Clyde R. Mark, "Israel: US Foreign Assistance" (Congressional Research Service, 2003).

23. Authors' calculations based on Office of Management and Budget, *Analytic Perspectives, Budget of the U.S. Government, Fiscal Year 2004* (2003), pp. 690–91.

24. Authors' calculations based on U.S. Census Bureau, "Current Population Projections" (2003) (www.census.gov/ipc/www/worldpop.html).

25. James Dobbins, John G. McGinn, Keith Crane, Seth G. Jones, Rollie Lal, Andrew Rathmell, Rachel Swanger, Anga Timilsina, "America's Role in Nation-Building: from Germany to Iraq" (Santa Monica, Calif.: RAND, 2003).

26. We are indebted to Susan Rice for insights in this section, especially related to reconstruction and humanitarian relief and contingency funds.

27. Average cost of reconstruction includes funds allocated to Iraq and Afghanistan, as well as to Bosnia and Herzegovina, Kosovo, the Federal Republic of Yugoslavia, Croatia, Macedonia, and Albania after U.S. and allied military operations in the region in 1999. Estimate assembled from a number of different sources: Lois B. McHugh and Joyce Vialet, "Kosovo: Refugee Assistance and Temporary Resettlement" (Congressional Research Service, 1999), p. 4; Bureau of Resource Management, "Congressional Budget Justifications: Foreign Operations, Fiscal Year 2004" (Department of State, 2003), available at www.state.gov/m/rm/rls/cbj; Bureau of Resource Management, "Congressional Budget Justifications: Foreign Operations, Fiscal Year 2003" (Department of State, 2002), available at www.state.gov/m/rm/rls/cbj; Bureau of Resource Management, "Congressional Budget Justifications: Foreign Operations, Fiscal Year

2002" (Department of State, 2001), available at www.state.gov/m/rm/rls/cbj; Kenneth Katzman, "Afghanistan: Current Issues and US Policy" (Congressional Research Service, 2003), pp. 35–36; Office of Management and Budget, "FY 2004 Supplemental: Iraq and Afghanistan Ongoing Operations/Reconstruction" (Office of Management and Budget, 2003), available at www.whitehouse.gov/ omb/budget/amendments/supplemental_9_17_03.pdf.

28. In fact, within the 2004 supplemental request submitted by the Department of Defense, we have identified over $1 billion in funding for activities related to humanitarian and disaster aid, reconstruction, counternarcotics activities, support for the Coalition Provisional Authority, and capabilities enhancement for local security forces. The $2 billion "Iraq Freedom Fund," with its own transfer authority, may also in part fund humanitarian and disaster assistance activities. Department of Defense, "FY2004 Supplemental Request for Operation Iraqi Freedom (OIF), Operation Enduring Freedom (OEF), and Operation Noble Eagle (ONE)" (September 2003).

29. Authors' calculations based on Office of Management and Budget, *Historical Tables*. Also see Isaac Shapiro, "As a Share of the Economy and the Budget, U.S. Development and Humanitarian Aid Would Drop to Post–WWII Lows in 2002" (Center on Budget and Policy Priorities, June 18, 2001).

4

Restructuring Domestic Spending

ISABEL SAWHILL AND
CHARLES SCHULTZE

This chapter discusses the domestic spending component of the better government plan. For purposes of the chapter, domestic spending consists of all budget outlays except defense, international affairs, homeland security, and the three large entitlement programs (Social Security, Medicare, and Medicaid), which are discussed elsewhere. In fiscal year 2003, domestic spending, apart from interest on the debt, accounted for 31 percent of the total budget and 6.3 percent of GDP. In our baseline budget these programs grow less rapidly than the economy, shrinking to 4.8 percent of GDP by 2014.

The better government plan is based on the premise that federal activities need continuous review as the economy changes and social norms evolve. When new national priorities gain acceptance, government is called on to devote resources to meet new objectives. But meanwhile, unfortunately, existing programs have acquired beneficiaries and political constituencies that make it almost impossible to cut them back. The benefits of such programs often go to a narrow segment of the population that is well organized to preserve its gains, whereas the costs are spread across a much larger population that has little incentive to evaluate the benefits or object to the higher taxes entailed. But if new programs are piled on top of old ones, the government will grow too large and unwieldy. Older programs should be periodically reviewed and some of them downsized or eliminated to make room for higher-priority spending.

We believe that effective government programs can both enhance the productivity of the economy and open opportunities for those left behind. The plan offers an illustrative menu of spending choices designed to move toward current national priorities in both areas. It rejects the view, inherent in the smaller government plan, that a substantial fraction of what the federal government does in the domestic arena is unwarranted. At the same time, it recognizes that over the years the budget has accumulated programs whose costs, at current funding levels, significantly outweigh their benefits and whose continued funding at those levels may slow economic growth. The plan includes a set of program cuts to make room for increases elsewhere. On balance, the program cuts and additions hold government spending relative to GDP at approximately its current level. The plan entails more revenue increases than spending cuts, however, because recent tax cuts have reduced revenues substantially below the GDP share that prevailed for several decades.

A detailed examination of the hundreds of individual domestic programs in the federal budget is beyond the scope of the current effort. This chapter simply illustrates the kinds of choices to be made if government is to be not just leaner but also better.

An Illustrative Menu of High-Priority Initiatives

Eliminating the deficit without addressing important domestic priorities would not make economic or social sense. Although a large continuing deficit is detrimental to economic growth, so is neglect of public investment in education, health, transportation, and research. Public investment complements private investment in new technologies, facilities, and equipment that enhance growth. Furthermore, citizens value such things as a cleaner environment, shorter commuting times, and safer streets, which enhance their quality of life but do not show up in conventional measures of economic welfare. Moreover, while most Americans have benefited from the higher productivity that has accompanied rapid advances in technology and globalization, some mechanism is needed to cushion the losses suffered by those whose jobs have been destroyed in the process. Restructuring the social safety net to encourage work can simultaneously increase the incomes of the least fortunate and produce more jobs and more growth. For all these reasons, a balanced plan to reduce the deficit should make room for new domestic spending to achieve these objectives.

This plan allocates roughly $21 billion a year for such purposes, in addition to increases in domestic spending already assumed in the base-line. Such a modest sum (less than 3 percent of total domestic discretionary spending) can make a substantial contribution to funding these new initiatives, although budgetary discipline will require making hard choices among competing priorities.

The first priority is "making work pay" by restructuring safety net programs to increase the incentives and rewards for low-wage workers. The reform of welfare in 1996 transformed the social policy landscape in the United States by requiring most mothers receiving welfare to work, limiting cash assistance to five years, and increasing state responsibility. These reforms have been far more successful than many people expected. Caseloads were more than halved. Child poverty declined. And the majority of mothers leaving welfare are working. Some of this success is due to the strong economy in the late 1990s, but much of it is due to new welfare rules in combination with more supports for low-wage earners that both encourage and reward work. These supports include the earned income tax credit, Medicaid, child care, and other programs that assist lower-income working families.[1]

Research suggests that further progress in reducing poverty and improving the life chances of children could be achieved by supporting the efforts of low-income parents to become self-sufficient through work. Work is a powerful antidote to poverty. If the heads of low-income families worked as much as the heads of nonpoor families, poverty in the United States would be almost halved.[2] But most former welfare recipients are single parents with little education or technical skill. The work available to them pays low wages and offers few benefits and little job security. To ensure that children are not left alone or in dangerous circumstances, a parent who is earning, say, $7 to $12 an hour needs help paying for child care.

Moreover, child care made affordable to low-income working families should not only ensure children's safety, but also help them develop the language and other skills they need for future success. The best Head Start and other early childhood development programs have well-documented track records of improving the later school success of disadvantaged children.[3] But Head Start and the Child Care and Development Block Grant program now serve only a fraction of the children eligible for assistance. Head Start targets preschool-age children from poor families and serves about 60 percent of eligible children.[4] The block grant targets all children in families with incomes up to $40,000 or $50,000 a year and serves only about 12 percent of those eligible.[5] Additional funding would enable more of the families eligible for assistance to participate.

A related priority is increasing health care coverage for low-income working families. An increasing number of low-wage jobs provide no health benefits. In recent years, considerable progress has been made toward covering low-income children through Medicaid or the Children's Health Insurance Program (CHIP). Even so, 20 percent of children in families below the poverty line were uninsured in 2002.[6] For their parents, the situation is even more serious. Although mothers on welfare are automatically eligible for Medicaid, once they leave the rolls for a job and have exhausted some temporary benefits, they often end up with no coverage at all, since only a third of low-wage workers have coverage through their employer.[7] Federal funds could be used to encourage states both to expand coverage under CHIP or Medicaid and to enroll more of those already eligible for these public programs.

Another priority is helping states improve elementary and secondary education—a key to future workforce productivity. Enactment of the No Child Left Behind Act of 2001 (NCLB) was a milestone in the many attempts to reform elementary and secondary education. The act combined an emphasis on standards and testing with new resources for teacher training, student assessments, preschool and after-school programs, and extra help for poor children. But some of the added funds earmarked for these purposes have never been appropriated, leaving states with a partially unfunded mandate to improve student performance on their own. In the meantime, states are struggling with the federal requirement to educate the increasing number of children with special needs, a requirement that absorbs as much as one-third of all education spending in some jurisdictions.[8]

Education is primarily a state and local responsibility, but NCLB reflected a national consensus that the federal government should help states increase the effectiveness of schools. To this end Washington should pick up the costs for the testing requirements of NCLB and assist states in meeting the "highly qualified" teacher components of the act. Teacher development is expensive, and although teacher training has historically been a state duty, NCLB requires that states raise certification requirements for secondary school teachers. Middle and high school teachers will have to demonstrate proficiency in the subjects they teach, either by having majored in the subject in college or by passing a test demonstrating college-level knowledge of the subject. In mathematics, approximately 50 percent of current teachers do not meet the requirement.[9] Without higher federal spending, the effort to improve educational outcomes and better prepare students for work is in jeopardy.

A final example concerns energy and the environment. Investments in less polluting or less energy-intensive products or manufacturing processes are public goods (meaning that those making the investments seldom get all the benefits for themselves). For this reason, clean and energy-efficient technologies are undersupplied by the market. An expansion of environmentally friendly research and development—without anointing any particular technologies as "the" solution—is clearly justified.

Such a goal need not impose new demands on the budget, however. Perhaps the most important step that could be taken to improve the environment and ease energy concerns would be to get the prices of energy right. Government could move the nation toward more accurate pricing either through taxes on energy or a system of auctioned and tradable emissions permits that confronts consumers with the full social cost of the energy they use, including environmental damages. Such measures could both reduce the deficit and encourage environmentally friendly research and investment.

Cutting Domestic Spending
(Outside Social Security, Medicare, and Medicaid)

The better government plan identifies domestic saving of several major types: federal investment and R&D programs that provide low or negative returns or that carry out activities better provided by the private sector; subsidy programs for business or for middle- and upper-income groups that do not provide public benefits commensurate with their costs; grants to state and local governments that do not meet the objectives for which they were established or that finance activities more properly financed by state and local taxpayers; and specific budget-saving improvements in the efficiency of government programs. Some of the savings identified here are also included in the sweeping cuts contained in the smaller government plan. But in keeping with the more positive view of the role of government underlying this plan, the criteria to select programs for spending cuts are substantially more selective than those applied in the smaller government plan.

In the remainder of the chapter, tables offer illustrative lists of spending cuts of various kinds included in the better government plan as they would affect fiscal 2014, the target year for eliminating the deficit. Together the cuts total $68 billion (table 4-1).[10] Even though these spending reductions are substantially smaller than those in the smaller government approach, many are quite controversial. Few cuts, however, can be made in existing federal programs without eliciting heated, if highly concentrated, opposition. And those unwilling to support the smaller government agenda sketched in chapter 2 must nevertheless recognize that without some significant spending cuts, neither deficit reduction nor attempts to fund new program initiatives will be acceptable to the broad public.

Finally, the presentation of such specific lists of cuts as those shown in the following tables does not imply a belief that any group of people, even those broadly supporting the same criteria as those used in constructing the tables, would select these particular reductions as the best choices available. The lists simply demonstrate that the spending objective in the better government plan could be met with those criteria in mind.

Table 4-1. *Better Government Plan: Illustrative Spending Cuts*
Billions of dollars

Category of cut	Cut in 2014
Subsidies	23
State and local grants	17
Low-value investment	20
Improved efficiency and reduction of fraud and abuse	8
Total	68

Sources and methods: Some savings from budget actions were identified by the authors, but many came from the Congressional Budget Office, *Budget Options* (March 2003), either directly, or as modified by the authors. In most cases the savings were estimated for fiscal 2003 and projected forward to 2014 at the same rate as the overall growth in discretionary spending in the baseline. In some cases, CBO projections of annual savings, available annually through 2008 and as five- and ten-year totals, were used as the basis for projecting 2014 estimates. Savings in mandatory programs were projected using CBO estimates of growth in those programs contained in its publication "The Budget and Economic Outlook: An Update," August 2003. Figures may not add to total because of rounding.

Federal Subsidies

In total, subsidy programs would be cut to produce $23 billion in annual budget savings by 2014 (see table 4-2). The largest of these cuts would come in farm subsidies.

Phasing down farm subsidies to half their current level for 2008 and subsequent years would save more than $6 billion a year by 2014.[11] Crop production in the United States is highly concentrated among large farms. Because subsidies are distributed among individual farms more or less in proportion to their production, the 7 percent of farms with gross receipts in excess of $250,000 in 2001 got 50 percent of all subsidy payments. Farmers with net income of $100,000 and over received an average of $50,000 each in subsidy payments.[12] There are limits on the payments that a farm can receive, but they are not fully effective—indeed one element of the subsidy system is explicitly constructed to bypass payment limits.

Supporters of large-scale farm subsidies argue that the current system is needed in good times and bad to keep small and intermediate-size farms, and a rural way of life, in existence. But the share of subsidies going to such farmers is small. Moreover, the excess production capacity sustained by U.S. farm subsidies depresses the livelihood of farmers in the third world. American subsidies, along with their European counterparts, are a major obstacle to world trade negotiations.

Table 4-2. *Subsidies: Illustrative Cuts*
Billions of dollars

Cut	Cut in 2014
Phase down farm subsidies to one-half baseline by 2008	6.5
Reduce selected conservation programs by half	1.3
Eliminate rural development programs (except housing)	1.2
Cut subsidy element for crop insurance in half	1.9
Phase out maritime subsidies by 2008	0.2
Charge fees for trade promotion	0.4
Eliminate advanced technology program and manufacturing partnerships	0.4
Eliminate Economic Development Administration, regional commissions, and related programs	1.2
Recover meat inspection costs with fees	1.0
Reform flood insurance to reduce subsidies and future flood damage	0.6
Eliminate Amtrak subsidies for less traveled lines	0.4
Eliminate veterans' disability compensation for disability ratings of 30 percent or less and use one-third of savings for higher disabilities	0.4
Charge FAA air traffic control fees based on marginal cost	2.0
Increase fees to cover 75 percent of additional transportation security costs	2.1
Charge fees for cost of operating inland waterways and levy harbor maintenance fees on port users	0.6
Charge 10 basis point fee per $100 of owned assets of Fannie Mae, Freddie Mac, and other government-sponsored housing enterprises	2.4
Charge market-based fees for power marketing administration sales	0.2
Eliminate requirement that government-owned or -financed cargo be carried on U.S. flag vessels	0.5
Total	23

Sources and methods: See table 4-1.

The smaller government program, which would wipe out all farm subsidies, goes too far. There is a legitimate case for federal income supports, within carefully defined limits, as a safety net. The better government program would restrict farm subsidies to countercyclical supports for farm families to offset some of the large declines in income which they periodically suffer because of the high volatility of agricultural prices. But even these subsidies should be subject to much lower payment limits.

In 1996, Congress enacted a substantially scaled-down subsidy system, only to pass a series of emergency measures sharply boosting subsidy levels a few years later. To ensure the permanence of the subsidy cut, such emergency appropriations should be prohibited under congressional procedures (see the discussion of budget procedures in chapter 2).

Other subsidy cuts are possible. Congress could, for example, impose a fee, based on marginal costs, for air traffic control services. The fees would vary by the cost of providing the services, which vary according to type of airport and other factors. Such fees would encourage a more efficient pattern of operations and yield savings of some $2 billion by 2014. Congress could also impose fees or raise highly subsidized charges for providing businesslike services. It could recover Department of Agriculture meat inspection costs with fees; reduce the subsidy for government-provided flood insurance, which often promotes development of frequently flooded areas; raise the fees for providing airline security; charge fees to exporters to cover costs of trade promotion activities; and cut in half the subsidy in government-sponsored crop insurance. Savings for 2014 would total $6 billion.

State and Local Grants

The smaller government plan for spending reductions wipes out some $123 billion of programs, principally federal grants to state and local governments, on grounds that there is no rationale for federal taxpayers to support programs that essentially meet the needs of citizens within individual state and local boundaries. Such programs, it posits, should therefore be the responsibility of state and local taxpayers. It consequently eliminates, among other programs, all grants for elementary and secondary education within the Department of Education; all housing subsidy, community development, and other grants of the Department of Housing and Urban Development; and the waste treatment grants of the Environmental Protection Agency. The better government plan cuts a substantial but much smaller $17 billion from federal grant programs (table 4-3).

One major difference between the two plans is that the better government approach preserves most or all grants that assist poor and disadvantaged households or schools and other institutions serving them. Competition among states and localities tends to limit the tax dollars those governments can devote to support for lower-income citizens and the institutions that serve them. The cost to state and local taxpayers for providing significant assistance to the poor and disadvantaged is twofold: the direct cost of the support itself and an indirect cost when generous provision of such services threatens to drive away well-to-do taxpayers or attract an influx of the poor from other jurisdictions. Partial support for

Table 4-3. *State and Local Grants: Illustrative Cuts*

Billions of dollars

Cut	Cut in 2014
Cut wastewater and drinking water construction grants in half by increasing state cost sharing	1.8
Eliminate senior community service employment program	0.6
Concentrate Community Development Block Grant funding on less wealthy communities	1.0
Eliminate federal grants for vocational and adult education, drug-free schools, and a number of additional purposes, while maintaining other grants such as those for disadvantaged schools and state grants for improving teacher quality	6.6
Combine twenty-four categorical grants into four block grants and cut totals by 10 percent	6.6
Total	17

Sources and methods: See table 4-1.

such services by the federal government reduces the competitive problem and lets taxpayers judge the merits of such programs more nearly on the basis of the direct cost of furnishing them.

In some cases, such as building interstate highways or constructing waste treatment plants along major rivers, the services provided by one governmental jurisdiction benefit in a substantial way citizens outside that jurisdiction. Here, federal grants that reimburse state and local governments for part of the cost of such services help make sure the services are indeed provided. The appropriate magnitude of such grants is, of course, a matter of budgetary policy.

Following these criteria, the better government plan preserves the housing subsidy grants of the Department of Housing and Urban Development that provide services to the poor and near-poor. Some might argue that the support furnished to lower-income citizens might be better served by lessening the fraction devoted to housing subsidies, but if so the funds saved should be rechanneled through other grants that serve the same population. The plan does not eliminate the Community Development Block Grant program but does recommend excluding more affluent communities from grant eligibility.

In addition to providing funds for elementary and secondary schools serving many children from disadvantaged families and for the No Child Left Behind initiative, the Department of Education oversees many other categorical grants to state and local governments for elementary and sec-

ondary education. Some grants provide modest funds for purposes that
are principally financed by and are a part of the educational responsibilities of state and local governments. Others fund special activities with
worthy objectives but limited effectiveness. Some, such as safe and drug-
free schools and vocational education, show few signs of improving outcomes.[13] And to the extent that the vocational curriculum successfully
meets the needs of particular communities, it is clearly in the interest of
those communities and their business establishments to support the program. Savings from eliminating these and other questionable programs
would amount to a little under $7 billion in 2014. The better government
budget plan does not, however, eliminate the program for the education
of the disadvantaged or a number of other major education grants.

The better government plan retains the Environmental Protection
Agency's grants for building waste treatment and water supply facilities,
but cuts them in half by increasing state cost sharing. It also proposes
combining twenty-four of the remaining federal grants into four block
grants and cutting their spending 10 percent. The increase in efficiency
and flexibility for the states ought, at least roughly, to make up for the
reduced funding. Grants for "income security" and those associated with
high-priority national objectives (for example, aid to disadvantaged
schools and state health insurance for children) were not included in the
group to be blocked.

Low-Value Federal Investments

Federal spending on low-value investments and research would be
reduced $20 billion a year by 2014 under the spending cuts suggested for
this category (table 4-4). Almost half the cuts would come in National
Aeronautic and Space Administration programs.

The space shuttle and the space station rank high on the list of major
federal investments whose costs have vastly exceeded the benefits deliv-
ered. Originally NASA's shuttle program was conceived as an inexpensive
way of sending human beings on numerous important military and scientific missions—as many as twenty-five to sixty missions a year.[14] But the
costs and complexity of life systems led to payload limits that sharply
downgraded the shuttle's usefulness. The Air Force dropped out as a cus-

Table 4-4. *Research and Investment Spending: Illustrative Cuts*
Billions of dollars

Cut	Cut in 2014
Eliminate manned space flight	9.0
Eliminate energy research on fossil fuels, solar and renewable sources, freedom car, conservation techniques, and grants to states for households	2.9
Eliminate construction grants for large and medium-sized airports	2.0
Eliminate earmarking in highway authorization bills	2.5
Eliminate grants for "light rail" urban mass transit investments	1.8
Reduce Army Corps of Engineers' new construction starts to the point where 2014 construction outlays, adjusted for inflation, are half of 2003 levels	1.3
Total	20

Sources and methods: See table 4-1.

tomer, and both military and serious scientific tasks have long been carried out through unmanned missions. By 1988, planned flights had dropped to eight a year; the past four years averaged five flights annually. Moreover, in the 113 shuttle flights launched to date, fourteen astronauts have died, an average fatality rate of one for every eight missions. The international space station is also vastly less productive than originally conceived. Because of spiraling costs and other problems, several design features were dropped and the planned crew size of seven was cut to three. Since substantial crew time is required simply to maintain the station, little capability is left for scientific uses. Phasing out both manned space flights and the space station would save a total of $9 billion by 2014.

Examples of other low-value investments that could be halted include the Energy Department's applied research on solar and renewable power sources, fossil fuels, and conservation technologies. The department would do better to concentrate on carrying out its basic research mission, for its record in developing commercially viable alternative sources of fossil fuels is poor. Markets for renewable power sources are growing rapidly, especially in photovoltaics and wind energy.[15] If the tax and tradable emissions permits recommended earlier are put in place, the private capital market should be able to support an expansion in applied research and development by private firms. A similar case can be made for reducing or eliminating the federal role in developing conservation technologies. However, the better government program leaves intact funds for general and more basic energy research. Such research is less likely to be supported through the incentives of the private market and is, unlike applied research, appropriately a federal function.

Congress could also eliminate its earmarked "high-priority" projects in the federal-aid highway program. Increasingly Congress requires that hundreds of specific highway projects be funded each year, on top of the regular federal-aid highway grants, whose use states decide subject to guidelines and broad categories established by the federal government. Essentially these earmarked projects are typical "pork barrel."

Congress could also reduce new construction starts by the Army Corps of Engineers to the point where outlays fall to something like 50 percent of their projected path. The smaller government program simply wipes out all funds for the corps' civil programs. Although the corps and its congressional supporters have often been criticized, with reason, for undertaking many projects whose realistically evaluated benefits cannot cover costs, one cannot assume that no water investments deserve federal support. The fraction of corps projects that would pass more rigorous cost-benefit evaluations may turn out to be higher or lower than assumed here, but significant budget savings can be expected. Funds for operating and maintaining existing corps inland waterway projects should be raised by fees on waterway users (included in the subsidy reduction category), thus relieving federal taxpayers of the need to subsidize waterway users. Together these proposals could save some $2 billion in 2014.

Improved Efficiency and Reduction of Fraud and Abuse

Congressional committees, the General Accounting Office, and agency inspectors general have reported numerous studies estimating losses of billions of dollars in erroneous, fraudulent, or excessively generous payments to individuals, health care providers, and business firms in general. And lists totaling scores of billions of dollars in potential budget savings have been compiled. Often, however, recommendations about how to achieve those savings are simply admonitory—"agency officials should work more closely with state and local enforcement officials," and so on. Enforcement efforts can indeed be improved and efficiencies are surely possible. But without highly specific and detailed plans and without much

Table 4-5. *Improving Efficiency and Reducing Waste: Illustrative Cuts*
Billions of dollars

Cut	Cut in 2014
Reform Medicare payment formula for home health care	4.5
Change Medicaid procurement rules to acquire drugs at competitive prices	0.8
Eliminate floor on rates for lenders fees on student loans	1.7
Improve FDA's list of approved brand-name drugs to speed the marketing of generic drugs	1.1
Total	8

Sources and methods: See table 4-1.

larger enforcement budgets and sometimes much more intrusive and time-consuming eligibility monitoring, one should not count on large budget savings.

In some cases the current "rules of the game" clearly foster excessive costs in the operation of government programs, and cost-saving changes can be made without creating onerous burdens for those involved. Annual savings amounting to $8 billion are identified in table 4-5. One example involves a change in the payment of home health care providers under Medicare. In 2001 the government, which had been paying these providers for each home visit to a patient, began the payment on the basis of a single charge for each sixty-day "episode" of care. A fee schedule per episode for each of eighty categories of treatment was set, taking into account the earlier experience about the specific services typically provided during a sixty-day period, But since then, home visits per episode have fallen by about one-third, and on average payments now exceed costs by 25 percent. The proposed reform would freeze episode payments for each of the eighty categories at the 2003 level through 2007, thus gradually narrowing the difference between costs and payments. Cost savings in 2014 would be in the neighborhood of $4 billion. (Medicare is the subject of chapter 5, but these savings involve administrative matters rather than payments to beneficiaries, and so are included here.)

Notes

1. Isabel V. Sawhill, Kent R. Weaver, Ron Haskins, and Andrea Kane, eds., *Welfare Reform and Beyond: The Future of the Safety Net* (Brookings, 2002), pp. 79–80.

2. Ron Haskins and Isabel Sawhill, "Work and Marriage: The Way to End Poverty and Welfare," Welfare Reform and Beyond Brief 28 (Brookings, September 2003).

3. Barbara Wolfe and Scott Scrivner, "Providing Universal Preschool for Four-Year-Olds," in Isabel Sawhill, ed., One Percent for the Kids (Brookings, 2003).

4. The percentage of income-eligible children who are enrolled in Head Start was computed by dividing the number of three- and four-year-old children served in 2001 by the number of three- and four-year-old children in poverty. For the former, see U.S. Department of Health and Human Services, Administration for Children and Families, Head Start Bureau, 2002 Head Start Fact Sheet, retrieved from www.acf.hhs.gov/programs/hsb/research/factsheets/02_hsfs.html. For the latter, see U.S. Bureau of the Census and Bureau of Labor Statistics, September 2002, Detailed poverty tables: 2001 P60 package, in Annual Demographic Survey: March Supplement, retrieved from ferret.bls.census.gov/macro/032002/pov/new23_001.html.

5. www.hhs.gov/news/press/2000pres/20001206.html.

6. Robert J. Mills and Shailesh Bhandari, "Health Insurance Coverage in the United States: 2002," Current Population Reports (U.S. Census Bureau, September 2003), p. 5.

7. Sara R. Collins and others, "On the Edge: Low-Wage Workers and Their Health Insurance Coverage," Issue Brief 626 (New York: Commonwealth Fund, April 2003), p. 6.

8. Pietro S. Nivola, Tense Commandments (Brookings, 2002), p. 9.

9. U.S. Department of Education, Office of Policy Planning and Innovation, "Meeting the Highly Qualified Teachers Challenge: The Secretary's Second Annual Report on Teacher Quality," 2003, p. 7.

10. Almost half of the total budget saving in table 4-1 comes from suggestions included in Congressional Budget Office, Budget Options (March 2003).

11. The CBO projection of "mandatory spending" assumes that farm subsidies will fall from the current $17 billion to $13 billion by 2013, despite a rise of some 20 percent in the general price level. While this kind of a fall seems quite unlikely, that level is built into the adjusted baseline projection used throughout this book and therefore controls the 2014 estimate of the size of the spending cut.

12. U.S. Department of Agriculture, Agricultural Income and Finance Outlook, AIS-79 (September 2002), table 9.

13. See evaluations in Congressional Budget Office, Budget Options, option 500-02, and Office of Management and Budget, Budget of the U.S. Government, 2004, pp. 93, 95, and 99.

14. See Cliff Letheridge, "History of the Space Shuttle Program," Spaceline, Inc., available at www.spaceline.org/rocketsum/shuttle-program.html.

15. See Congressional Budget Office, Budget Options, option 270-03, p. 62.

5

The Impact of an Aging Population

HENRY J. AARON AND
PETER R. ORSZAG

Balancing the budget over the next decade is an important goal for the nation in part because later decades threaten to bring even larger budget challenges. The first baby boomers become eligible for early Social Security retirement benefits in 2008 and for Medicare in 2011. As the baby boomers increasingly become eligible for these programs, the federal budget is expected to begin running deficits vastly larger than those projected over the next decade.[1]

Balancing the budget by 2014 will help prepare both the economy as a whole (through higher national saving, which raises our future productivity) and the federal budget (through smaller increases in public debt, which reduce future debt service costs) to meet these challenges. Merely balancing the budget over the next decade, however, is not enough. Both Social Security and Medicare face long-term deficits. The sooner both are placed on a solid long-term footing, the better it will be both for the federal budget and for program beneficiaries. Both programs are a major source of long-term budget imbalance, and early action will allow changes to be implemented gradually and spare everyone the burden of abrupt tax increases or benefit cuts. Delay carries the threat that sudden and dramatic changes in benefits on which people had based their retirement plans may one day be forced on us.

Avoiding abrupt changes to the major retirement programs implies not only that long-term reforms should be enacted as soon as possible, but also that sound long-term reforms will contribute little to balancing the federal budget over the next decade. The fiscal benefits will eventually be enormous, but most will come much later. For example, many Social Security reform plans, reflecting a commitment not to cut benefits of current retirees or older workers, maintain benefits for those fifty-five or older.[2] Those younger than fifty-five in 2004 will not become eligible for Social Security retirement benefits until after 2011 and will receive only about 5 percent of the total retirement benefits paid between 2005 and 2014. The potential contribution to budget balance over the next decade from a long-term reform that, as we believe proper, exempts retirees and near-retirees is therefore small.

In any case, the focus of this book is how to eliminate the deficit in the unified budget over the next decade. It will not address the much larger and more complex problems of how to restore long-term financial balance to Social Security and Medicare and whether and how to change their structure. Nor will it address the quite different but equally serious issues in the design of Medicaid, the federal-state program that provides health benefits for the poor. We believe that large-scale modifications in Social Security and Medicare should be designed not to achieve near-term savings, but rather to improve the structure of retirement and health programs for the aged and disabled and to place them on a sound long-term footing. For these reasons, we make no attempt to evaluate or indicate our preferences among alternative long-term Social Security and Medicare reforms.[3] We list several in tables later and indicate the generally small contribution they can make to balancing the unified budget in the next decade.

Background on Entitlement Spending

In 2004, mandatory spending—outlays that do not require an annual congressional appropriation—is projected to total $1.3 trillion, more

Table 5-1. *Projected Social Security, Medicare, and Medicaid Outlays as a Percentage of GDP, 2004–60*

Percent

Year	Social Security	Medicare	Medicaid	Total
2004	4.3	2.6	1.6	8.5
2010	4.3	3.2	1.8	9.3
2015	4.8	3.5	2.1	10.4
2020	5.4	4.5	2.4ᵃ	12.3
2040	6.6	6.7	4.0	17.3
2060	6.8	8.4	5.2	20.5

Source: Congressional Budget Office, "The Budget and Economic Outlook; An Update," August 2003; and U.S. House of Representatives, Committee on Ways and Means, *2000 Green Book, Background Material and Data on Programs within the Jurisdiction of the Committee on Ways and Means,* October 6, 2000.

a. Assumes that Medicaid spending rises at the same rate as projected Medicare outlays.

than half of all government spending. Of this mandatory spending, about three-fourths will go for the "Big Three"—Social Security, Medicare, and Medicaid.

Spending on these three programs is projected to grow rapidly as the baby boom generation ages—nearly doubling as a share of gross domestic product by 2040. If, as is commonly assumed, per capita medical spending continues to outpace growth of per capita GDP even after 2040, the budget shares will keep on growing (table 5-1). Furthermore, both Social Security and one of the two major parts of Medicare—hospital insurance, or part A—are financed through dedicated taxes that, over the long term, are projected to be insufficient to pay for all benefits promised under current law.

Social Security

Social Security is now running a sizable cash-flow surplus—more than $164 billion in 2004. The excess of revenues over outlays for benefits and administration is projected to grow until it reaches almost $334 billion in inflation-adjusted dollars in 2015. Revenues include payroll taxes, now 12.4 percent of earnings up to a ceiling ($87,900 in 2004), most of the income tax collections on Social Security benefits, and interest on accumulated reserves. Pension costs will rise fast as the baby boomers become eligible for retirement benefits. Projections indicate that these revenues and accumulated reserves—now $1.5 trillion—will be sufficient to pay for currently legislated benefits through 2042. The same projections indicate that earmarked revenues will cover 95 percent of promised Social Security benefits over the next fifty years and 88 percent over the next seventy-five years.[4]

Medicare

Medicare hospital insurance (HI, or part A) is also running cash-flow surpluses—$24 billion in 2004. Benefits, which include inpatient hospital care, skilled nursing facility care, home health care, and hospice care, are financed by a payroll tax of 2.9 percent of all earnings and part of income tax collections on Social Security benefits received by the upper-income elderly and disabled. These surpluses are projected to grow and remain around $35 billion for the next decade. Accumulated surpluses are projected to cover all currently promised benefits through 2026.

The long-term deficit in HI is proportionately much larger than that in Social Security. Dedicated revenues and accumulated reserves are projected to cover only 71 percent of promised benefits over the next fifty years and 58 percent over the next seventy-five years. The Medicare projections are subject to more uncertainty than are those for Social Security. Both are subject to demographic and economic contingencies, but Medicare projections also depend sensitively on growth of *per capita* health care costs.

Medicare supplemental medical insurance (SMI, or part B) covers doctors' services, a few outpatient drugs and vaccines, durable medical equipment, and certain other services. Premiums paid by Medicare eligibles cover about one-fourth of program costs, and general revenues cover most of the rest. Under legislation enacted in 2003, premiums will be increased for upper-income enrollees, starting in 2007. The same legislation expands coverage of out-patient drugs, starting in 2006. The cost of SMI, already a sizable current drain on the budget, is projected to grow rapidly. Outlays net of premiums paid by enrollees are projected to rise from $95 billion in 2004 to $163 billion in 2012. In addition, the drug benefits and other changes in Medicare will absorb $58 billion in general revenues in 2012 and more in succeeding years.

Medicare expenditures are expected to rise even faster than pension costs because outlays will be driven not only by the growing ranks of beneficiaries, but also by per capita medical costs that are projected to increase faster than per capita income.

Medicaid

Medicaid pays for acute and long-term care for the poor—elderly and nonelderly—and for premiums, deductibles, and cost sharing under Medicare for people enrolled in both programs. Because most middle-class Americans have few savings apart from Social Security and home equity, many quickly exhaust their assets and become eligible for Medicaid when old and forced to enter nursing homes. Medicaid accounts for more than 40 percent of all nursing home and home health payments. In recent years, Medicaid outlays have risen much faster than Medicare spending. The recent recession has simultaneously inflated Medicaid rolls and forced states to cut back on services and eligibility to hold down costs. Over the long term, Medicaid costs could rise faster or slower than Medicare outlays. The exact pace will depend not only on the number of aged and disabled (as do Medicare outlays) but also on changes in the proportion of the population that is in poverty and on state policies.[5]

Clearly, in the case of all three programs, specific long-term estimates matter little because it is impossible accurately to project economic and demographic conditions and health technology decades into the future. But these projections leave little doubt that Social Security faces a long-term deficit, probably of modest size and manageable if tackled soon, but increasingly difficult to handle if action is long delayed. The projections also show that Medicare hospital insurance faces a huge and challenging deficit and that supplemental medical insurance, the new prescription drug benefits, and Medicaid will impose increasing burdens on general revenues.

Entitlement Reform and the Federal Budget

Social Security, Medicare, and Medicaid constitute a large and growing part of the budget. To exclude them entirely from the effort to restore fiscal balance would make achieving that goal all the more difficult. In addition, as emphasized above, long-term reform should ideally be enacted soon to spread the burden of addressing the long-term funding problems confronting both Social Security and Medicare hospital insurance.

At the same time, it makes little sense to base big changes in the nation's core retirement programs on short-term budget savings rather than on long-term structural considerations. Congress has never been willing to enact large, abrupt cuts in either Social Security or Medicare. Sound policy as well as politics explains this reticence.

Congress has, however, made small benefit cuts with little notice, and we propose some below. For example, in 1983 Congress cut Social Security benefits to help deal with a current cash-flow deficit and a projected long-term deficit. Congress enacted an immediate implicit benefit reduction of less than 2 percent, but it delayed implementing a much larger long-term benefit cut (raising the age at which benefits can be claimed) for seventeen years and then spread the ensuing cuts over two six-year periods, one from 2000 through 2005 and one from 2017 through 2022. Thus, Congress allowed nearly four decades from enactment until full implementation. This degree of gradualism underscores the caution with which Congress has handled benefit changes within the key retirement programs. By contrast, tax increases or general revenue transfers can be implemented with less notice because they mostly affect workers, who are better positioned than retirees to adapt to such policy changes.

Social Security Reform

Despite the constraints imposed by the bipartisan and sensible agreement to phase in slowly any significant benefit changes to the program, Social Security can contribute to the goal of eliminating the deficit in the unified budget over the next decade. Below, we describe three changes—two plans to take into account the costs of increasing life expectancy and one plan to improve inflation adjustments—that would reduce the unified budget deficit significantly over the next decade. All three changes are consistent with a variety of long-term reforms in Social Security. Table 5-2 shows how such changes would affect federal expenditures in 2014.

OFFSETTING INCREASING LIFE EXPECTANCY. The lifetime value of Social Security old age benefits is the expected value of benefits from the

Table 5-2. *Proposed Savings from Reforms in Social Security in 2014*
Billions of dollars

Reform	Saving
Accelerate increase in full benefits age to offset costs of increasing life expectancy	1.4
Adjust benefit formula to offset half the costs of increasing life expectancy	<1.0
Improve adjustment for inflation	17.0
Total	19

Source: Authors' estimates.

age of claiming until death. As life expectancy increases, the generosity—and cost—of the system automatically increases. One way to hold down costs is to reduce annual benefits to offset the increased duration of benefit payment as life expectancy increases.[6]

Congress took a step in this direction in 1983 when it increased from sixty-five to sixty-seven the age at which "full" benefits are paid. (Benefits are actuarially raised or lowered if workers claim benefits after or before the "full" benefits age.) The first of these increases—from age sixty-five to sixty-six—will be complete in 2005. The second step—from sixty-six to sixty-seven—is not scheduled to begin until 2017. Several reform plans have proposed accelerating this shift, which is ultimately equivalent to a benefit cut of about 7 percent for those who will be affected by the change in timing.

The Social Security Commission appointed by President Bush in 2001 recognized that benefit cuts for those soon to retire are neither politically acceptable nor sound policy. Specifically, the commission proposed no cuts in retirement benefits promised under current law for any worker aged fifty-five or older. Because the age of initial eligibility is sixty-two, the commission's stance amounts to a refusal to endorse benefit cuts affecting workers within seven years of initial eligibility. Accepting that phase-in period, one could accelerate the benefit cuts enacted in 1983 and now scheduled to begin in 2017; these reductions could instead begin in seven years—that is, in 2012. In other words, the full benefit age could begin increasing again in 2012 rather than 2017. Accelerating this increase would contribute savings in the period 2005–14 of $2.4 billion ($1.4 billion in 2014).

Another way to respond to increasing longevity would be to adjust the benefit formula each year to offset at least part of the cost-increasing effects of rises in life expectancy. Starting such adjustments in 2012, as proposed in a recent Brookings volume, *Saving Social Security*, would produce negligible savings between 2005 and 2014—less than $500 million—but would save far more in the future than would a one-time increase in the full benefits age to sixty-seven because the benefit formula would be adjusted continually as life expectancy increases over time.[7]

IMPROVING INFLATION ADJUSTMENTS. For more than three decades, both political parties have endorsed the principle that Social Security benefits should be fully protected from inflation. To achieve that goal, benefits have, since 1972, been automatically adjusted to keep pace with the consumer price index (CPI). Analysis has revealed that the CPI somewhat overstates growth in the cost of living for the population as a whole.[8] The Bureau of Labor Statistics has created an alternative price index, C-CPI-U, which more accurately measures the cost of living. Federal Reserve Board Chairman Alan Greenspan, among others, has proposed using this alternative measure to index Social Security.

Such a change would reduce benefits for retirees and near-retirees but could nonetheless be justified by the generally accepted principle that the real purchasing power of currently payable benefits should be maintained. Switching to the C-CPI-U would reduce Social Security benefit costs by an estimated $70 billion cumulatively from 2005 through 2014 ($17 billion in 2014). (It could also increase personal income tax collections by an estimated $83 billion from 2005 through 2014, $18 billion in 2014, and reduce other public spending by several billion dollars more.)

Although some critics oppose this change on the ground that the elderly have different spending patterns from those of the general population, that the real purchasing power of retirement benefits should increase over time with rising productivity, and that the change imposes the largest relative burdens on those who live the longest, several technical adjustments made recently to the official CPI have reduced measured inflation without eliciting opposition. Switching to a more accurate price index should be no more objectionable than correcting the current index.

RESTORING LONG-TERM BALANCE OF THE CURRENT SYSTEM. In table 5-3 we list several proposals advanced in recent years either to change the long-term structure of Social Security or to close projected long-term Social Security deficits. Most would somewhat reduce Social

Table 5-3. *Elements of Long-term Plan to Restore Financial Balance to Social Security*
Billions of dollars

Element	Change in 2005–14	Change in 2014
Benefit changes		
Adjust benefit formula to offset half the costs of increasing life expectancy, starting in 2012	<1	<1
Accelerate increase in full benefits age (from age 66 to 67) from 2017–22 to 2012–17	2	2
Reduce benefits as a share of average earnings for workers with earnings exceeding $64,000, starting in 2012	<1	<1
Extend period over which average earnings are computed to establish initial benefits from 35 to 38 years, starting in 2008	2	1
Revenue changes		
Increase earnings base to include 90 percent of all earnings; for further explanation, see chapter 6	470	53
Cover newly hired state employees, starting in 2008	55	14
Impose a 3 percent payroll tax ("legacy tax") on all earnings over the Social Security earning ceiling to cover the cost of benefits paid to past and current beneficiaries in excess of the value of their and their employers' payroll taxes, starting in 2005	296	38
Raise the payroll tax by 0.3 percent each on workers and employers (from a total of 12.4 percent to 13 percent) in 2005	358	44
Treat Social Security benefits like private pension benefits for tax purposes by including in income subject to personal income tax all Social Security benefits in excess of employees' payroll taxes	185	40

Source: Authors' estimates.

Security spending or increase revenues. All would retain primary reliance on a defined-benefit pension system.[9] Several would have large long-term effects, but none reduces spending much over the next decade.

Many of these proposed changes are controversial, and no consensus has yet emerged on whether or how to close the projected financial deficit within the current system. Should such a consensus develop soon, these proposals could also help close a small part of the unified budget deficit over the next decade. Most of the spending reductions or revenue increases would nonetheless occur outside the ten-year budget window that frames all of the proposals presented in this book.

DIVERTING SOCIAL SECURITY REVENUE TO INDIVIDUAL ACCOUNTS. President Bush appointed his Social Security Commission to

Table 5-4. *Elements of Long-term Plan to Divert Social Security Revenue to Individual Accounts*
Billions of dollars

Element	Change in 2005–14	Change in 2014
Adjust income ranges to which various replacement rates apply by changes in prices rather than changes in wages for retirees reaching age 62, starting in 2012	2	2
Divert 2 percentage points of the payroll tax from Social Security into individually owned private accounts for workers age 55 or younger, starting in 2005	–1,300	–152

Source: Authors' estimates.

honor his presidential campaign pledge to have such a commission recommend ways to replace Social Security in part with individually owned
investment accounts. The commission duly reported, on December 11,
2001, and presented three plans, all of which would have allowed workers to divert a portion of the payroll tax from Social Security to individual investment accounts.

President Bush did not endorse any of these plans. In the current budget situation it is extremely unlikely that he, or the winner of the 2004
election, will—or should—do so, regardless of the long-term strengths or
weaknesses of these proposals. The reason is that if implemented, all three
plans would greatly aggravate the unified budget deficit not only for the
next ten years (table 5-4), but for many years more. They would do so
because each would reduce revenues far more than benefits for several
decades. By 2040, each plan would have increased the government debt
in the hands of the public by more than $4 trillion (for comparison, debt
in the hands of the public at the end of fiscal year 2003 was nearly
$3.8 trillion).

Almost any plan to divert Social Security revenue into individual
accounts will add to, not relieve, government deficits over the medium
term, as long as it protects benefits for current retirees and those nearing
retirement. The reason is that traditional Social Security benefit payments
would continue *and* the federal government would also have to find funds
to deposit in the newly created, individually owned accounts.

These deposits would either boost spending or divert federal revenue.
In either case, they would increase the budget deficit for many years. It

would take several decades before cuts in traditional benefits linked to individual accounts would offset the diversion of revenue itself.

Medicare and Medicaid Reform

Will Rogers once reviewed a restaurant by commenting that the food was mediocre and there wasn't enough of it. Much the same can be said of Medicare, with the addition that it is also very expensive. It exposes beneficiaries to high cost sharing. It does not limit total out-of-pocket costs during serious and extended illnesses. And it does not cover nursing home costs, other than those in a skilled nursing facility immediately following hospitalization.

Although coverage is below the standard of employment-based insurance, Medicare hospital insurance is still projected to cost far more than the taxes earmarked to pay for it. And the costs of supplementary medical insurance (part B), in excess of the 25 percent of program outlays covered by premiums, are projected to claim ever growing shares of general revenues. In brief, even with its inadequate benefits, Medicare is likely to pose massive fiscal challenges.

The shortcomings in Medicare's coverage make it difficult to see how significant reductions in growth of benefits would be politically feasible in the coming years. Indeed, if anything, pressure for expanding the program is likely to increase. The debate on the recently enacted prescription drug bill was a vivid lesson. That bill added well over $500 billion to the budget deficit over the next decade (including added interest costs) and close to $2 trillion to the deficit over the succeeding decade.[10] We are persuaded that in evaluating such potential expansions in Medicare, policymakers should always recognize the trade-offs with other areas of the budget. Medicare benefits should not be increased without offsetting spending reductions or tax increases. In other words, the PAYGO principle, which chapter 2 recommends for all mandatory spending, should be applied.

Requiring beneficiaries to shoulder more of the cost of covered services through premiums, deductibles, and other forms of cost sharing is an option that merits increased scrutiny. Few current Medicare beneficiaries have paid premiums approaching the actuarial value of the benefits they receive.[11] Shifting some of Medicare's costs to patients through increased cost sharing or higher premiums would reduce long-term budget costs. It is unclear, however, whether such charges would be sufficient to offset any added long-term cost of extending Medicare benefits.

Whatever other structural changes may eventually be made in Medicare, some savings are possible over the next decade through targeted changes, including increased charges on enrollees. Table 5-5 shows how such changes in Medicare would affect federal revenue in 2014.

SMI PREMIUMS. When Medicare was enacted in 1965, Congress set the premiums for supplementary medical insurance to cover half of program costs. The other half was to come from general revenues. The principle of automatic adjustments for inflation had not yet been applied to any major government program. (Social Security benefits, as noted, were first automatically indexed to inflation in 1972.) Thus, Medicare premiums were initially fixed and had to be changed by legislation. But Congress failed to raise premiums as fast as program costs grew. In 1972, it limited premium growth to the increase in the consumer price index, which was rising far more slowly than *per capita* SMI costs. Over time, premiums came to cover less than one-fourth of program costs. In the 1980s Congress overrode its own limit on premium increases to hold premiums at one-fourth of total SMI costs and in 1997 it set the premium at this level.[12]

Some subsidy of supplemental medical insurance premiums is desirable to encourage the elderly and disabled to enroll in SMI. Deep subsidies for the low-income elderly are justified to spare them from having to divert their meager incomes to pay health insurance premiums. In fact, federal and state governments jointly cover all premiums (and many other Medicare charges as well) for elderly and disabled beneficiaries who qualify for and receive Medicaid. But some premium increase for the majority of current supplementary medical insurance enrollees can be justified as part of a program to restore fiscal balance.

The 2003 bill that introduced drug coverage took a tiny step in this direction by reducing the premium subsidy over five years starting in 2007. For married Medicare enrollees with incomes from $160,000 to $200,000 (single enrollees with incomes of $80,000 to $100,000), the subsidy would be reduced from 75 percent to 65 percent. The subsidy

Table 5-5. *Proposed Savings from Reforms in Medicare and Medicaid in 2014*

Billions of dollars

Reform	Savings
Increase supplemental medical insurance premium	16
Reform indirect teaching payments	5
Reduce overpayments to managed care plans	5
Reform upper-payment limit	0
Reform and reduce payments to disproportionate share providers	2
Total	28

Source: Authors' estimates and Congressional Budget Office, *Budget Options* (March 2003).

reduction would be progressively larger as income rises, dropping from 75 percent to 20 percent for couples with annual incomes of $400,000 or more (single enrollees with incomes of $200,000 or more). These increases would initially affect only about 3 percent of Medicare beneficiaries (rising to 6 percent when fully implemented).

As part of a program to lower the deficit, the premium subsidy could be lowered from 75 percent to 65 percent for all Medicare beneficiaries, effective in 2005.[13] If one-third of the additional revenues were used to protect low-income Medicare beneficiaries from the premium increase and to provide aid to states whose Medicaid budgets will skyrocket as baby boomers increasingly become eligible for long-term care, this measure would reduce net spending by $123 billion during 2005–14 and by $16 billion in 2014.

INDIRECT TEACHING PAYMENTS. Medicare increases payments to teaching hospitals in recognition of the extra costs they are thought to incur because they provide more tests and other procedures and to care for particularly sick patients. Some extra compensation for such costs is in order. But the Medicare Payment Advisory Commission has found that the current bonus is roughly twice as large as it should be to compensate teaching hospitals for added costs. Cutting the payments over a three-year period starting in 2005 to half of their levels under law in effect before the drug bill was enacted would lower total Medicare spending by an additional $40 billion over the period 2005–14 and $5 billion in 2014.

PAYMENTS TO MANAGED CARE. Medicare now pays managed care plans more than the costs it incurs though traditional Medicare. The reimbursement rate is 103 percent of the average cost in each county. Before 1997, managed care plans received 95 percent of the average cost of serving Medicare patients in each county. This rate enabled taxpayers to gain savings that managed care plans were supposed to generate and to capture savings the plans reaped from enrolling healthier-than-average patients. Currently, managed care plans enroll patients who cost about 16 percent less than the average enrollee. Although a new formula is supposed to adjust payments based on expected costs, the methodology is imperfect and accounts for only a small fraction of potentially predictable cost variation. Because the gain is large, managed care plans are likely to continue to try to attract low-cost patients and there is probably no pricing formula that will prevent them from doing so. Rather than trying to narrow the current unwarranted subsidies to managed care, the 2003 drug bill added to them by increasing payments by nearly $16 billion from 2005 through 2014 ($2 billion in 2014). At a minimum, this increase could be rescinded and managed care plans be paid no more than 100 percent of the average cost of treating Medicare patients. These steps would shave an estimated total of $38 billion from Medicare spending from 2005 through 2014 and $5 billion in 2014.[14]

UPPER-PAYMENT LIMIT. The federal government pays each state a fraction of the state's cost of services provided to Medicaid enrollees. Allowable costs cannot exceed what Medicare would pay them. This ceiling is called the "upper-payment limit." In practice, however, Medicaid's payments are typically smaller than Medicare's. This difference created an opportunity for states to cook the books to extract more from the federal government. A transaction by Pennsylvania is illustrative. In 2000, twenty counties borrowed $695.6 million from a bank. They then transferred it to the state Medicaid agency's account in the same bank.[15] The Medicaid agency then made a grant of $697.1 million (the original amount plus a $1.5 million fee) to the counties, ostensibly as payment for treating Medicaid patients. The counties used the proceeds to pay off the loan. The state then billed the federal government $393.3 million—the federal matching share (56.4 percent) of its "outlay" of $697.1 million—and used this sum for other purposes.

To curb such abuse, Congress authorized and the Department of Health and Human Services imposed regulations that take effect gradually through 2008. Accelerating the effective date to 2006 would reduce spending faster but would have no effect on outlays in 2014 as the new regulations are projected to be fully in effect in our baseline.

DSH PAYMENTS. Medicaid provides extra payments to states for services rendered by hospitals that serve a disproportionate share of Medicaid patients (hence the acronym, DSH). A justification for such payments is that hospitals serving many Medicaid patients are likely also to provide disproportionate amounts of uncompensated care to uninsured patients. Thus, payments based on the numbers of Medicaid (and Medicare) patients can help hospitals serve the uninsured without weakening their incentives to collect reimbursements whenever possible.

Although some form of assistance may well be justified, the distribution of assistance under the current DSH program is badly flawed. Current rules permit states to extract large sums with gimmicks similar to those used to exploit the upper-payment limit. Because not all states have used this option, the pattern of DSH payments bears little relation to the problem they are intended to ameliorate. In 1997, for example, DSH payments per Medicaid or uninsured individual ranged from more than $500 in five states to less than $10 in eight states. The larger totals come in part from the clever use of payments to providers that the states recover in other ways but that form the basis of claims against the federal government. Some of the funds advance the intended purpose of extending health care to the uninsured, but some—an estimated 40 percent of the $7 billion annual cost in the late 1990s—flow back to state treasuries as general government support.

Successive administrations of both parties have proposed limits on DSH payments to curb these abuses. Congress has been willing to cap payments, but not to reform the fundamental structure of the program. The stated objectives of the program would be better achieved if the federal government established standards for direct allocation of funds to hospitals and other qualifying facilities that serve poor or uninsured populations. Given states' current fiscal duress, no immediate cutbacks in DSH payments—or any other form of federal assistance to the states—should be made. Starting in 2006, though, DSH payments could be channeled directly to caregiving facilities and total spending scaled back 20 percent. The net saving would be between $15 billion and $20 billion from 2006 through 2014.

Summary

Some analysts and elected officials have claimed that serious discussion of budget deficits cannot begin until people acknowledge that spending on "entitlements"—usually defined to include Social Security, Medicare, and Medicaid—must be cut by large amounts. We believe this view is flawed. Well-designed reforms of these entitlement programs will eventually produce large savings and are essential for long-term fiscal balance, but one should not expect substantial budgetary savings over the next decade. On Social Security, for example, the unwillingness to cut pensions for retirees or those soon to retire is bipartisan and close to unanimous. This reticence is well founded. Medicare outlays are unlikely to be cut significantly even in the long run, given justifiable pressure to liberalize a rather parsimonious benefit package.

Finally, growth of state revenues slowed or stopped in the recent recession, forcing significant cutbacks in Medicaid coverage. Further curtailments in Medicaid coverage would threaten to destroy the only health coverage available to millions of poor Americans. For that reason, we think that reductions in Medicaid spending beyond what we have outlined in this chapter are undesirable.

Notes

1. Congressional Budget Office, "A 125-Year Picture of the Federal Government's Share of the Economy, 1950 to 2075," Long-Range Fiscal Policy Brief 1 (June 14, 2002, revised July 2002).

2. The Commission to Strengthen Social Security appointed by President George W. Bush recommended that benefits not be changed for current beneficiaries or workers fewer than seven years from eligibility. This standard is also adopted in other recent Social Security reform plans.

3. For our views on reforming Social Security, see Peter A. Diamond and Peter R. Orszag, *Saving Social Security: A Balanced Approach* (Brookings, 2004). For an earlier set of recommendations, see Henry J. Aaron and Robert R. Reischauer, *Countdown to Reform: The Great Social Security Debate* (Century Foundation, 2001). For views on reforming Medicare, see Henry J. Aaron and Robert R. Reischauer, *Modernizing Medicare for the 21st Century* (Century Foundation, forthcoming).

4. Present tax rates would be sufficient to pay 73 percent of scheduled benefits after the trust fund is projected to be exhausted in 2042 and 65 percent of scheduled benefits in 2077.

5. Growth will also depend on legislation. For example, the law adding a drug benefit to Medicare also terminated federal support for Medicaid payments for drugs on behalf of people who are also eligible for Medicare.

6. Increasing the age at which retirement benefits can first be claimed, currently age 62, has virtually no effect on long-term costs. The reason is that monthly benefits are increased for each month that a person defers claiming benefits, up to age 70, when benefits are paid automatically. These adjustments compensate those who delay claiming benefits with a benefit increase that is computed actuarially to approximately offset the reduced period over which benefits will be paid. Increasing the age at which benefits may be claimed would have large effects on budget outlays over the next decade, however, because all of the "front-end" savings from deferred payment would be realized but few of the added costs from increased monthly payments would be incurred. We do not include this change as a means of financing deficit reduction because counting as savings a reduction in current outlays, when there is no reduction in long-term cost, would be dishonest.

7. The plan in Diamond and Orszag, *Saving Social Security*, offsets roughly half the cost of increases in life expectancy through gradual benefit reductions and roughly half through payroll revenue increases.

8. The Bureau of Labor Statistics has made various adjustments to reduce that bias. The CPI on which Social Security indexation is based, however, has failed to incorporate the fact that when relative prices change, consumers typically shift away from major categories of goods that have become more costly and toward categories of goods that have become less expensive.

9. Chapter 6, which lists changes in tax laws that could contribute to deficit reduction, also includes several tax increases that would help sustain the current surpluses in Social Security. Again, most of the revenue gains occur after 2014.

10. Authors' estimate.

11. This statement will cease to be universally true in the future, as the 2.9 percent payroll tax levied for Medicare hospitalization benefits (part A) has since 1993 applied to all earnings. For a small proportion of high earners, therefore, the actuarial value of taxes will exceed the actuarial value of benefits.

12. Committee on Ways and Means, U.S. House of Representatives, *2000 Green Book, Background Material and Data on Programs within the Jurisdiction of the Committee on Ways and Means*, October 6, 2000.

13. In practice, supplemental medical insurance premiums are subtracted automatically from monthly Social Security benefit checks. Most beneficiaries would see these premium increases simply as a cut in cash pensions.

14. Rolling back payments to 95 percent of average cost would lower spending by $70 billion from 2005 through 2014 and $11 billion in 2014. So large a cut is probably unjustified, as one motivation for setting the payment at 95 percent of average cost was recognition that managed care plans were enrolling

patients with lower-than-average costs, the very problem that risk-adjusted premiums aim to offset, even if they succeed only imperfectly.

15. This example is reported by Andy Schneider and David Rousseau, "Upper Payment Limits: Reality and Illusion in Medicaid Financing," Kaiser Commission Issue Paper (February 2002).

6

Meeting the Revenue Challenge

HENRY J. AARON, WILLIAM G. GALE, AND
PETER R. ORSZAG

B etween 2000 and 2003, federal revenue fell from 20.8 percent of the economy to 16.5 percent, its lowest share since 1959. Although revenue will increase as a share of GDP as the economy recovers from the recent recession, it will remain insufficient to match spending needs under any of the plans sketched earlier in the volume.[1] As a result, all of those plans will require higher taxes if the budget is to be balanced by 2014.

This chapter is a guide to revenue options that would help balance the budget. Accordingly, we present a menu of options for revenue increases from which policymakers and citizens could choose. For the most part, these changes are simple adjustments to tax rates or the tax base, but we also include rough estimates of added revenues from new forms of taxation. Although we refer to the changes as revenue increases, many are increases only relative to the adjusted baseline laid out in chapter 1. Compared with the official tax code, which assumes that the tax cuts enacted in 2001, 2002, and 2003 will expire in 2010 or before, most of the changes represent *tax reductions*.

To avoid turning this chapter into a book of its own, we do not examine in any detail many of the broader issues crucial to evaluating the effects of tax changes, including the impact on equity, simplification, or economic growth. But it is worth noting that well-designed revenue increases can make taxes both more equitable and simpler.

Although most tax increases are thought to discourage economic activity, revenue increases can also help, or at least not hurt, economic efficiency and growth. Taxes have two sets of effects on the economy. First, they directly shape economic decisions, including work behavior, saving, investment, and risk taking. Available evidence suggests these effects are usually modest and occasionally positive. For example, higher tax rates on items, such as cigarettes, that create social costs can reduce economic distortions, as can closing loopholes. Second, revenue increases have a positive indirect effect. By reducing the budget deficit (or raising the surplus), revenue increases can raise national saving—the sum of private and public saving—which in turn raises the future national income of American households. The net impact of tax changes is the sum of the direct and indirect effects. In short, whether tax increases support or hamper economic growth depends, in large measure, on how they are designed.[2]

Historical evidence shows no clear correlation between tax rates and economic growth. The United States has enjoyed rapid growth both when taxes were low and when taxes were high. The strongest recent extended period of growth in U.S. history spanned the two decades from the late 1940s to the late 1960s, when the top marginal personal income tax rates were 70 percent or higher. Economic growth accelerated after the top marginal tax rate was increased from 31 percent to 39.6 percent in 1993.[3] Comparisons across countries confirm that rapid growth has been a feature of both high- and low-tax nations. These considerations suggest that well-designed revenue increases need not inflict significant damage and may even strengthen economic performance.

To provide some perspective on possible tax changes, we note that in 2003 the federal government collected nearly $1.8 trillion in revenue. Individual income taxes supplied almost half the total (see table 6-1). Another 40 percent came from payroll taxes earmarked to finance social insurance programs, primarily Social Security and Medicare. Corporate income taxes and such other revenue sources as estate and gift taxes, excise fees, and customs duties accounted for the remainder.

Table 6-1. *Sources of Federal Revenue, Fiscal Year 2003*

Source	Billions of dollars	Percent of revenue	Percent of GDP
Individual income tax	794	44.5	7.4
Social insurance taxes	713	40.0	6.6
Corporate income tax	132	7.4	1.2
Other	144	8.1	1.3
Total	1,783	100.0	16.6

Source: Congressional Budget Office, "Monthly Budget Review," October 9, 2003, and authors' calculations.

Potential Revenue Sources

How much revenue is required to achieve budget balance in 2014 depends on how much the nation spends. According to the adjusted baseline, the budget deficit in 2014 is $687 billion, or about 3.7 percent of GDP (see chapter 1). The three plans set forth in chapter 2 would close, respectively, 25 percent, 75 percent, and all of the gap through tax increases.[4]

We examine seven types of tax changes:

—partial or full repeal or expiration of the 2001, 2002, and 2003 tax cuts;

—reform of the alternative minimum tax;

—increases in payroll taxes earmarked for Social Security;

—increases in excise taxes, such as those on cigarettes and alcoholic beverages;

—technical changes that would collect additional revenue;

—base-broadening, including scaling back current tax expenditures; and

—new revenue sources, such as a permit-trading system on carbon emissions or a value-added tax.

Adjusting the 2001, 2002, and 2003 Tax Cuts

In 2001 and 2003, President Bush requested and Congress approved large tax cuts—the Economic Growth and Tax Relief Reconciliation Act of 2001 and the Jobs and Growth Tax Relief Reconciliation Act of 2003. These acts reduced marginal tax rates, increased the child credit, pro-

Table 6-2. *How Would Repealing the 2001–03 Tax Cuts Affect Federal Revenue in 2014?*

Change	Billions of dollars	Percent of GDP
1. Reverse all 2001 income tax changes (exclude alternative minimum tax and capital gains/dividends changes)	262	1.4
2. Reverse 2001 income tax changes that benefit high-income filers (return top four marginal rates to 2000 levels)	79	0.4
3. Retain estate tax		
At a 35 percent tax rate with $5 million exemption per person	30	0.2
At a 45 percent tax rate with $3.5 million exemption per person	38	0.2
At a 50 percent tax rate with $2.5 million exemption per person	46	0.3
4. Repeal capital gains, dividends tax reductions from 2003 act given change #1	39	0.2
5. Eliminate bonus depreciation provisions in 2002 act	29	0.2
6. Reform alternative minimum tax		
Given changes #1 and #4	38	0.2
Without changes #1 and #4	70	0.4

Source: Authors' calculations based on Tax Policy Center microsimulation results and published Joint Committee on Taxation and Congressional Budget Office estimates.

vided marriage penalty relief, gradually eliminated the estate tax, and made numerous other changes. Under the 2001 act, many of these provisions were phased in slowly over time. The 2003 act accelerated the reductions in marginal tax rates and some other provisions enacted in 2001 whose implementation was delayed. The 2003 act also reduced taxes on capital gains and dividends. All or some of these cuts could be reversed (see table 6-2).[5]

One revenue-increasing option involves reversing the income tax changes made in 2001, including all of the marginal tax rate reductions, the child credit increases, and marriage penalty relief. This option raises $262 billion in 2014, or about 1.4 percent of GDP relative to the adjusted baseline.[6]

A second option would reverse only the income tax cuts that benefit primarily high-income filers. If cuts in tax rates primarily affecting lower- and middle-income filers—the increase in the child credit from $500 to

$1,000, the creation of a 10 percent marginal tax bracket, and the marriage penalty relief provisions included in the 2001 legislation—are retained and only those cuts that affect the 25 percent of tax units who face marginal rates above 15 percent are undone, revenues would increase by about $80 billion in 2014. Under this option, the roughly 75 percent of tax units in the zero, 10 percent, or 15 percent marginal rate brackets would continue to enjoy all the tax cuts they received under the 2001 act. Higher-income households would still receive tax cuts, though these would be smaller than the cuts originally legislated.

The 2001 act also called for the gradual reduction and eventual elimination of the estate tax. In 2001, that tax fell on estates with a net value (after allowable deductions, including unlimited transfers between spouses and charitable gifts) of more than $600,000. The maximum estate tax rate was 55 percent. The 2001 act raised the estate-value floor gradually to $3.5 million in 2009 and lowered the maximum rate to 45 percent. At this level, the tax would apply to only 5 decedents in 1,000—approximately 10,000 estates each year nationwide. The 2001 act repealed the estate tax in 2010 but restored pre-2001 law in 2011. Retaining the estate tax under the terms that apply in 2009, with the ceiling adjusted annually for inflation, would raise about $38 billion in 2014 relative to repealing it altogether. Applying the tax to estates with a net value of $2.5 million or more per person with a maximum rate of 50 percent would raise $46 billion relative to the adjusted baseline. Taxing only estates of $5 million or more per person at a maximum rate of 35 percent would increase revenue by $30 billion in 2014.

A fourth option would rescind the cuts in taxes on dividends and capital gains enacted in 2003. These tax cuts do not efficiently address the stated goal of eliminating the "double taxation" of corporate income. Double taxation refers to the fact that corporate profits are taxed once through the corporation income tax and again at the personal level through personal income tax on dividends and capital gains.[7] We and many other economists believe that all corporate income should be taxed once—but *only* once—at the same rate that applies to labor income received by any given taxpayer. Today some corporate source income is taxed twice, but some escapes tax altogether, through shelters or because of corporate tax subsidies.[8] The provisions of the 2003 act regarding dividends and capital gains address the first problem, but not the second. This "dessert now, vegetables later" approach, which addresses only half the problem, reduces the chances of dealing with the whole. The dividend and capital gains tax cuts could be repealed and legislation could be enacted that prevents both double taxation and no taxation in a revenue neutral way. Following this course would raise revenues by almost $40 billion in 2014.[9]

The final option in this section is to eliminate the 50 percent "bonus depreciation" provision for business investments introduced in the 2002 tax cuts and extended in the 2003 legislation. This provision was intended to provide a temporary stimulus to business investment during the recession, not to serve as a permanent subsidy.[10] Eliminating it would raise $29 billion in 2014 relative to the adjusted baseline.

Reform the Alternative Minimum Tax

The individual alternative minimum tax (AMT) was originally designed to collect taxes on filers who aggressively sheltered their income. All taxpayers must pay the regular income liability or the AMT, whichever is larger. For most filers, the AMT is so low that they need not bother with it. Only 2.4 million people now pay the AMT. Because the ordinary income tax is adjusted for inflation but the AMT is not, the number of filers subject to the AMT will grow rapidly to 33 million by 2010. Our adjusted baseline assumes that the AMT is modified so that it is indexed for inflation and otherwise reformed to prevent more filers being subjected to it (see chapter 1).

Even while preventing a substantial increase in the share of taxpayers on the AMT, revenue-increasing reforms are possible. For example, one could keep the total share of taxpayers on the AMT roughly constant, while shifting AMT liabilities higher up the income distribution. One such option would raise the top AMT tax rate to 35 percent, repeal the AMT exemption phase-out, treat dividends and capital gains as ordinary income under the AMT (so that the preferences for capital gains would remain in the ordinary income tax but not in the AMT), and raise the real value of the AMT exemption over time. This option would also raise $38 billion in 2014 if the income tax rate reductions and capital gains and dividends tax cuts were repealed and about $70 billion if they were retained (see table 6-2).[11]

Increasing Social Security Revenue

As noted in chapter 5, Social Security faces a long-term financial shortfall that will have to be resolved by some combination of benefit cuts and tax increases. The payroll tax that finances Social Security is now 12.4 percent on earnings up to a ceiling—$87,900 in 2004. In 1983, when the last major congressional legislation on Social Security was enacted, the ceiling covered 90 percent of all earnings in covered employment. The earnings ceiling is adjusted annually for growth in average wages. Since 1983, however, earnings inequality has grown. As a result, the share of earnings subject to payroll tax has fallen from 90 percent to 85 percent.

We include three options for boosting revenues through an increase in the ceiling on taxable earnings and one for increasing the tax rate (see table 6-3). Increasing the ceiling so that the payroll tax covers 87 percent of earnings—about halfway between the current level and the one that applied in 1983—would raise revenues in 2014 by $21 billion and would require raising the ceiling in 2004 to about $105,000. Covering 90 percent of earnings would require raising the ceiling to about $130,000 in 2004; it would boost revenues in 2014 by $53 billion. Eliminating the ceiling and subjecting all earnings to the 12.4 percent payroll tax would raise $158 billion in 2014 alone and, if made permanent, would eliminate the seventy-five-year deficit in Social Security. These revenue estimates are all based on an unchanged tax rate of 12.4 percent. Raising the payroll tax rate from 12.4 percent to 13.0 percent without raising the ceiling would raise $44 billion in 2014 and close roughly one-third of the projected seventy-five-year deficit in Social Security.

Another option is to impose a charge to offset the loss of Social Security reserves resulting from past decisions to pay early cohorts more in benefits than their contributions could have financed.[12] If earlier cohorts had received only the benefits that could have been financed by their contributions plus interest, current Social Security reserves would be larger and better able to finance future benefits. This gap comprises a "legacy debt," which must be financed in the future. A 3 percent "legacy charge"

Table 6-3. *How Would Raising Social Security Taxes Affect Federal Revenue in 2014?*

Change	Billions of dollars	Percent of GDP
Raise earnings ceiling so that 87 percent of total earnings are taxable	21	0.11
Raise earnings ceiling so that 90 percent of total earnings are taxable	53	0.29
Eliminate earnings ceiling so that all earnings are taxable	158	0.85
Raise payroll tax rate to 13 percent	44	0.24
Impose 3 percent legacy charge on earnings above ceiling	38	0.20

Source: Authors' calculations based on Congressional Budget Office, *Budget Options* (March 2003), and data from the Office of the Chief Actuary, Social Security Administration.

on earnings above the existing payroll tax ceiling would raise about $40 billion in 2014. It would also close approximately a third of the seventy-five-year deficit in Social Security.

Increases in "Sin" Taxes

Certain taxes, such as those on cigarettes and alcohol, discourage the use of products that impose social costs. For example, the cigarette tax discourages smoking and reduces smoking-related disease. An increase in this tax would strengthen this disincentive, particularly for teenagers, whose limited incomes and typically brief addiction make their smoking decisions more sensitive to the price of cigarettes than are those of adults. Consequently, an increase in the excise tax on tobacco would be particularly effective in discouraging teen smoking.[13] Similarly, taxes that raise the price of alcohol discourage drinking, even among heavy drinkers.[14] Raising the excise tax on cigarettes by 50 cents a pack would increase revenue by an estimated $7 billion in 2014 (see table 6-4).[15] Increasing the tax on all alcoholic beverages to a standardized $16 per proof gallon—which would raise the tax on a six-pack of beer from 33 cents to 81 cents—would raise $6 billion.

Activities that create pollution also impose costs on society. Accordingly, a third option in this category is to raise the gas tax. Increasing this tax by 12 cents a gallon, from 18.4 cents to 30.4 cents a gallon, would

Table 6-4. *How Would Expanding "Sin" Taxes Affect Federal Revenue in 2014?*

Change	Billions of current dollars	Percent of GDP
Increase excise tax on cigarettes by 50 cents a pack	7	0.04
Increase taxes on alcohol to $16 per proof gallon	6	0.03
Increase gas tax by 12 cents a gallon	20	0.11

Source: Authors' calculations based on Congressional Budget Office, *Budget Options* (March 2003).

Table 6-5. *How Would Technical Changes in the Tax System Affect Federal Revenue in 2014?*

Change	Billions of dollars	Percent of GDP
Index the tax code to the improved consumer price index	18	0.1
Improve enforcement	37	0.2

Source: Authors' calculations based on Tax Policy Center microsimulation results and Leonard Burman, Testimony before the Committee on Ways and Means, U.S. House of Representatives, July 17, 2003.

raise $20 billion in 2014, reducing the deficit, encouraging fuel efficiency, and curtailing pollution.

Technical Changes

Two technical changes in the revenue system would also help to reduce the deficit (see table 6-5). The first involves the price index used to adjust personal exemptions, the standard deduction, and the income levels at which tax rates change. These nominal quantities are adjusted annually according to changes in the consumer price index to hold them constant in real terms. Research has shown that the consumer price index overstates inflation somewhat. As a result, personal exemptions and the standard deduction tend to grow in real value, and revenues are lower than they would be if the index were more accurate than it is. As explained in the chapter on entitlements, the Bureau of Labor Statistics has developed a so-called superlative price index that measures inflation better than does the traditional consumer price index. Using the improved index in the future would reduce measured inflation by an estimated 0.2 percentage point a year and raise revenue in 2014 by $18 billion.

A second technical change would deal with the disturbing fact that many taxpayers simply do not pay the taxes they owe. One reason is that the Internal Revenue Service lacks the resources to enforce payment. Providing the IRS with an additional $2 billion a year to collect the taxes people owe would reduce the deficit by approximately $37 billion by 2014.[16]

Base-broadening Options

Broadening the tax base generates additional revenue with no increase in statutory tax rates. It can also improve economic efficiency by reducing tax-motivated distortions between similar activities.

At the personal level, the current tax system favors foreign earned income. Each American who lives and works abroad can qualify for an exclusion from income taxation of up to $80,000 of earnings. This provision originated when few American worked abroad and it served as a crude offset to taxes U.S. foreign residents were assumed to owe abroad. However, people receive the exclusion from U.S. taxation even if they owe no foreign tax. Eliminating the exclusion, so that all income earned abroad would be included in taxable income in the United States, would raise $5 billion in 2014 (see table 6-6). U.S. foreign residents would still be eligible for a credit for foreign taxes paid, so that they would not be taxed twice on their income.

At the business level, the United States is going to have to make changes in its very low tax rates on so-called Foreign Sales Corporation/Extra-Territorial Income (FSC/ETI). The World Trade Organization has found these rates to be export subsidies, which are prohibited by international treaty. The European Union has been authorized to impose billions of dollars in trade sanctions on U.S. exports if the FSC/ETI tax provisions are not repealed. Bipartisan support exists for repealing the FSC/ETI, a step that would raise revenue by an estimated $7 billion in 2014. Unfortunately, Congress is debating which of a long list of alternative tax breaks it should link to repeal of the prohibited subsidies, reducing revenues rather than raising them.

Table 6-6. *How Would Base-Broadening Options Affect Federal Revenue in 2014?*

Change	Billions of dollars	Percent of GDP
Eliminate foreign earned income exclusion	5	0.03
Repeal FSC/ETI	7	0.04
Replace mortgage interest deduction with 15 percent tax credit	36	0.20

Source: Authors' calculations based on Tax Policy Center microsimulation results, Congressional Budget Office, *Budget Options* (August 2003), and Joint Committee on Taxation.

Current tax rules subsidize homeownership by permitting homeowners to deduct mortgage interest. This deduction is a subsidy because the homeowner/investor is not required to report an estimate of the investment income (or "imputed" rent) on the same investment. Under current law, taxpayers may deduct interest paid on up to $1 million of mortgage loans. This deduction favors high-bracket filers because the tax saving is proportional to one's marginal tax rate and because high-bracket filers tend to live in much more costly houses than do low-income households. Transforming the home mortgage interest deduction into a refundable 15 percent credit would have a number of advantages. It would encourage homeownership among filers whose incomes put them in the 10 percent marginal rate bracket and those with incomes too low to require tax payments. It would be helpful or neutral for the three-quarters of tax units facing the 15 percent or lower marginal tax brackets. And it would raise revenue in 2014 by $36 billion, which would come from added taxes on the 25 percent of filers who face marginal rates above 15 percent.

Other Revenue Options

Rather than relying on the personal or corporation income tax to generate increased revenue, Congress might decide to create new revenue sources. Most developed nations and all members of the European Union now impose a value-added tax (VAT)—a tax collected at each stage of production that amounts to a tax on consumption unless goods and services are expressly shielded from tax.[17] Many observers believe that par-

Table 6-7. *How Would New Tax Options Affect Federal Revenue in 2014?*

Change	Billions of dollars	Percent of GDP
Impose VAT, excluding small businesses, education, religion, and health care:		
2 percent rate	149	0.8
5 percent rate	372	2.0
8 percent rate	632	3.4
Create carbon trading system, assume $25 per ton permit price	34	0.2

Source: Authors' calculations.

tially replacing the income tax with a VAT would promote saving because the VAT taxes consumer purchases.

A broad-based VAT (one that excludes only small businesses, education, religion, and health care) would generate revenue of about 0.4 percent of gross domestic product for each 1 percentage point of tax. It would also increase the cost of government purchases. The net contribution to deficit reduction, therefore, would be 0.4 percent of GDP—or $74 billion in 2014—for each 1 percentage point of tax (see table 6-7). A VAT could be imposed at a low rate—say, 2 percent—as part of a larger tax program. At 5 percent, the revenue would close almost 70 percent of the deficit in 2014. At 8.5 percent, a VAT would more than close the entire adjusted baseline deficit in 2014.

Another option—a tax on carbon emissions, combined with a market in rights to emit carbon—would deal with a major environmental problem as well as contribute to deficit reduction. This program would reduce greenhouse gas emissions and the harm caused by global climate change.[18] Total carbon emissions would be capped. Companies would need a permit to emit carbon.[19] Each year the government would auction permits authorizing the emission of carbon at the capped level. As an illustration, suppose that the number of carbon permits were set equal to the number of tons of carbon emitted in 1990. Suppose further that the permit price turned out to be $25 per ton of carbon. At that price and quantity, the auctions would raise $34 billion in 2014. Taking into account the increase in prices paid by the government, the net revenue increase would amount to 0.2 percent of GDP.[20]

Packages

The options presented above can be combined in various ways. In considering which items to choose, policymakers and citizens should evaluate not only how much revenue the proposals produce, but also how the burdens are distributed and how they affect economic activity. For example, repealing the income tax cuts from the 2001 legislation or retaining the estate tax would burden upper-income taxpayers more and lower-income taxpayers less than would imposing a value-added tax or increasing sin taxes.

Tables 6-8, 6-9, and 6-10 present three revenue packages. The smaller government package closes 25 percent of the adjusted baseline deficit in 2014; the better government package closes 75 percent; and the larger government package closes more than 100 percent. Clearly, it would be possible to raise the same amounts with other packages. These changes represent large tax increases from the perspective of the adjusted baseline. But if the various expiration dates ("sunsets") for tax cuts in current law were allowed to take effect, revenues would be $548 billion higher in 2014 than in our adjusted baseline. Thus, if one takes current law as the basis of comparison rather than our adjusted baseline, the plans that close 25 percent and 75 percent of the deficit in 2014 via tax increases do not represent tax increases but tax *cuts* of $400 billion and $150 billion, respectively, and the plan that relies exclusively on tax increases to close the deficit in 2014 would represent a revenue increase of $80 billion, or about 0.4 percent of GDP.

Table 6-8. *How Would the Smaller Government Package (25 percent of Deficit Reduction from Revenue) Affect Federal Revenue in 2014?*

Change	Billions of dollars	Percent of GDP
Reform alternative minimum tax	70	0.4
Retain estate tax at a 35 percent tax rate with $5 million exemption	30	0.2
Improve enforcement	37	0.2
Total	137	0.7

Table 6-9. *How Would the Better Government Package (75 Percent of Deficit Reduction from Revenue) Affect Federal Revenue in 2014?*

Change	Billions of dollars	Percent of GDP
Return top four marginal rates to 2000 levels	79	0.4
Retain estate tax with $3.5 million exemption	38	0.2
Improve enforcement	37	0.2
Index tax code to improved consumer price index	18	0.1
Repeal 2003 capital gains and dividends tax reductions	39	0.2
Reform alternative minimum tax	38	0.2
Raise Social Security earnings ceiling so that 90 percent of earnings are taxable	53	0.3
Eliminate bonus depreciation	29	0.2
Raise payroll tax rate to 13 percent	44	0.2
Create modest carbon trading system	27	0.1
Total	402	2.2

Table 6-10. *How Would the Larger Government Package (100 Percent of Deficit Reduction from Revenue) Affect Federal Revenue in 2014?*

Change	Billions of dollars	Percent of GDP
Return top four marginal rates to 2000 levels	79	0.4
Retain estate tax with $3.5 million exemption	38	0.1
Improve enforcement	37	0.2
Index tax code to improved consumer price index	18	0.1
Repeal 2003 capital gains and dividends tax reductions	39	0.2
Reform alternative minimum tax	38	0.2
Eliminate Social Security earnings ceiling so that all earnings are taxable	158	0.9
Eliminate bonus depreciation	29	0.2
Raise payroll tax rate to 13 percent	44	0.2
Impose a 2 percent value-added tax	149	0.8
Total	629	3.4

Notes

1. Under our adjusted baseline, the tax cuts are extended beyond their official sunsets. Under that baseline, revenue increases from 16.5 percent of GDP in 2003 to 17.6 percent in 2013—which is below its average level over the past several decades and, more important, well below projected spending.

2. For further discussion, see William G. Gale and Samara R. Potter, "An Economic Evaluation of the Economic Growth and Tax Relief Reconciliation Act of 2001," *National Tax Journal*, vol. 55 (March 2002).

3. Some may argue that economic growth would have been even more rapid, and pretax income gains among top earners even more dramatic, were it not for the 1993 marginal tax rate increases. But the evidence to support such a proposition is weak, and on its face it seems implausible.

4. In all cases, the sum of spending cuts and tax increases is smaller than $687 billion because deficit reduction means slower growth in the public debt and in attendant interest outlays than would result if deficits increase unabated.

5. Again, it is worth emphasizing that if current law is followed, all of these tax cuts will have expired by 2014.

6. This estimate is relative to the adjusted baseline. It is based on results from a model devised by the Tax Policy Center, a joint project of the Urban Institute and the Brookings Institution. The results were reduced by 20 percent to reflect an estimate of the effects of the microeconomic behavioral responses likely to be assumed by congressional revenue and budget scorers. The Tax Policy Center model generates revenue estimates that are completely "static" (that is, they do not incorporate any behavioral reaction to the tax changes). The 20 percent reduction factor is intended to roughly match published estimates from the congressional Joint Committee on Taxation or the Congressional Budget Office, which incorporate microeconomic responses to the tax changes. The same 20 percent reduction factor is applied to the revenue estimate for repealing only the top four marginal rate reductions.

7. For further explanation, see Leonard E. Burman, William G. Gale, and Peter R. Orszag, "Thinking Through the Tax Options," *Tax Notes* (May 19, 2003).

8. Robert McIntyre, "Calculations of the Share of Corporate Profits Subject to Tax in 2002," Citizens for Tax Justice, January 2003.

9. This estimate is based on extrapolations of the Congressional Joint Committee on Taxation estimates.

10. The bonus depreciation provision, by allowing 50 percent immediate expensing, also distorts incentives to invest in assets with long depreciation lives relative to assets with short depreciation lives. The revenue estimate is based on extrapolations of the Congressional Joint Committee on Taxation estimates.

11. The top statutory marginal tax rate under the AMT is now 28 percent, but the phase-out of the exemption under the AMT raises the effective marginal tax rate to 35 percent. After the exemption is fully phased out (in 2003, when alternative minimum taxable income is slightly less than $400,000 for married filers), the effective marginal tax rate declines back to 28 percent. This option would eliminate the phase-out of the exemption but raise the marginal tax rate to 35 percent. As a result, the effective rate would rise only for those now above the exemption phase-out range. The revenue estimate is based on results from the Tax Policy Center model.

12. Peter A. Diamond and Peter R. Orszag, *Saving Social Security: A Balanced Approach* (Brookings, 2004).

13. See, for example, Jonathan Gruber, "Youth Smoking in the U.S.: Prices and Policies," Working Paper 7506 (Cambridge, Mass.: National Bureau of Economic Research, January 2000). Disagreement exists about whether the current ciga-

rette excise tax adequately reflects the costs imposed by smokers on others; a new line of research emphasizes instead the costs imposed on the smoker himself and why the initial decision to smoke may not have been made with adequate information about the future consequences. For discussion, see David Cutler and Jonathan Gruber, "Health Policy in the Clinton Era," and W. Kip Viscusi, "Comments," in Jeffrey A. Frankel and Peter R. Orszag, eds., *American Economic Policy in the 1990s* (MIT Press, 2002). Gruber has also shown that smoking imposes costs on less-than-fully-rational decisionmakers that justify cigarette taxes far higher than any now imposed. See Jonathan Gruber and Botond Koszegi, "A Theory of Government Regulation of Addictive Bads: Optimal Tax Levels and Tax Incidence for Cigarette Excise Taxation," Working Paper 8777 (Cambridge, Mass.: National Bureau of Economic Research, February 2002).

14. See David Cutler, "Public Policy for Health Care," in A. Auerbach and M. Feldstein, eds., *Handbook of Public Economics*, vol. 4 (New York: North-Holland, 2002).

15. These revenue estimates are based on extrapolations from Congressional Budget Office, *Budget Options* (March 2003), revenue options 33–35.

16. Leonard E. Burman, Testimony before the Committee on Ways and Means, United States House of Representatives, July 17, 2003.

17. For more detailed discussion of the economic effects of a VAT, see Henry J. Aaron and William G. Gale, eds., *Economic Effects of Fundamental Tax Reform* (Brookings, 1996).

18. For ways of designing incentives to mitigate climate change, see Joseph E. Aldy, Peter R. Orszag, and Joseph E. Stiglitz, "Climate Change: An Agenda for Global Collective Action," Pew Center on Global Climate Change, October 2001.

19. A "safety valve" system in which the government would commit to selling permits at a given price, even if the result is that the quantity target is exceeded, has advantages over a strict quantity-based system. See William Pizer, "Choosing Price or Quantity Controls for Greenhouse Gases," Resources for the Future, Climate Issues Brief 17 (1999), and Warwick J. McKibbin and Peter J. Wilcoxen, "Climate Change after Kyoto: A Blueprint for a Realistic Approach," *Brookings Review*, vol. 20 (Spring 2002).

20. If transition relief were granted to the most affected parties and were inclusive of the effect on government purchases, the net effect on revenue would be reduced. For various methods of providing transition relief and the costs involved, see Congressional Budget Office, "Shifting the Cost Burden of a Carbon Cap-and-Trade Program," July 2003.

Budgeting for National Priorities
Advisory Board

External Advisers

KENNETH M. DAM
Max Pam Professor of American and Foreign Law, University of
    Chicago Law School
Deputy Secretary, Department of Treasury, 2001–03
Deputy Secretary, Department of State, 1982–85
Executive Director, Council on Economic Policy, 1973
Assistant Director for National Security and International Policy, Office
    of Management and Budget, 1971–73

MARIO DRAGHI
Managing Director, Goldman Sachs
Executive Director, World Bank, 1984–90
Director General, Italian Treasury, 1991–2001

WILLIAM FRENZEL
Senior Fellow, Brookings Institution
Member, U.S. House of Representatives (R-Minnesota), 1971–91
Ranking Minority Member, House Budget Committee and House
    Administration Committee
Member, House Ways and Means Committee
Member, President's Commission to Strengthen Social Security, 2001

LEE H. HAMILTON
Director, Woodrow Wilson International Center for Scholars
Member, U.S. House of Representatives (D-Indiana), 1965–99
Chairman, Vice Chairman, and Member, Joint Economic Committee

JACOB J. LEW
Executive Vice President, New York University
Director, Office of Management and Budget, 1998–2000

JAMES T. LYNN
Retired CEO, Aetna Life and Casualty Co.
General Counsel, Department of Commerce, 1969–71
Undersecretary, Department of Commerce, 1971–73
Secretary, Department of Housing and Urban Development, 1973–75
Director, Office of Management and Budget, 1975–76

DAVID MAXWELL
Retired Chairman and CEO, Fannie Mae
General Counsel, Department of Housing and Urban Development,
    1970–73

RUDOLPH G. PENNER
Senior Fellow, Urban Institute
Director of the Congressional Budget Office, 1983–87
Assistant Director for Economic Policy, Office of Management and
    Budget, 1975–77
Deputy Assistant Secretary for Economic Affairs, Department of
    Housing and Urban Development, 1973–75
Senior Staff Economist, Council of Economic Advisers, 1970–71

JOHN PORTER
Partner, Hogan and Hartson, LLP
Member, U.S. House of Representatives (R-Illinois), 1980–2001
Member, House Appropriations Committee
Chairman, House Subcommittees on Labor, Health and Human
    Services, and Education
Vice-Chairman, Subcommittee on Foreign Appropriations

LAURA D. TYSON
Dean, London Business School
Chairman, Council of Economic Advisers, 1993–97

MURRAY WEIDENBAUM
Professor, Washington University, St. Louis
Chairman, Council of Economic Advisers, 1981–82
Member, President Reagan's Economic Policy Advisory Board, 1983–89

JOHN WHITEHEAD
Chairman, Lower Manhattan Development Corporation
Deputy Secretary, Department of State, 1985–89
Chairman, Federal Reserve Bank of New York, 1996–2000

Senior Staff

HENRY J. AARON
Senior Fellow, Brookings Institution
Assistant Secretary for Planning and Evaluation, Department of Health,
 Education, and Welfare (Carter administration)
Chair, Advisory Council on Social Security, 1979
Member, Institute of Medicine

LAEL BRAINARD
Senior Fellow, Brookings Institution
Deputy National Economic Adviser and Deputy Assistant to the
 President for International Economics (Clinton administration)
Special Assistant to the President and Senior Director for International
 Economic Policy
Personal Representative (Sherpa) of the President to the G7/8

WILLIAM G. GALE
Senior Fellow and Deputy Director of Economic Studies, Brookings
 Institution, and Codirector, Brookings-Urban Tax Policy Center
Senior Staff Economist, Council of Economic Advisers, 1991–92

RON HASKINS
Senior Fellow, Brookings Institution
Senior Adviser to the President for Welfare Policy at the White House,
 2001
Majority Staff Director, Subcommittee on Human Resources, Commit-
 tee on Ways and Means, U.S. House of Representatives, 1995–2000
Welfare Counsel, Republican Staff, Subcommittee on Human
 Resources, Committee on Ways and Means, U.S. House of Represen-
 tatives, 1986–94

MICHAEL E. O'HANLON
Senior Fellow, Brookings Institution
Defense and Foreign Policy Analyst, National Security Division,
 Congressional Budget Office, 1989–94

Index

Ᏸ THE BROOKINGS INSTITUTION

The Brookings Institution is an independent organization devoted to nonpartisan research, education, and publication in economics, governance, foreign policy, and the social sciences generally. Its principal purposes are to aid in the development of sound public policies and to promote public understanding of issues of national importance. The Institution was founded on December 8, 1927, to merge the activities of the Institute for Government Research, founded in 1916, the Institute of Economics, founded in 1922, and the Robert Brookings Graduate School of Economics and Government, founded in 1924. The Institution maintains a position of neutrality on issues of public policy. Interpretations or conclusions in Brookings publications should be understood to be solely those of the authors.